THE BOOK OF GALWAY

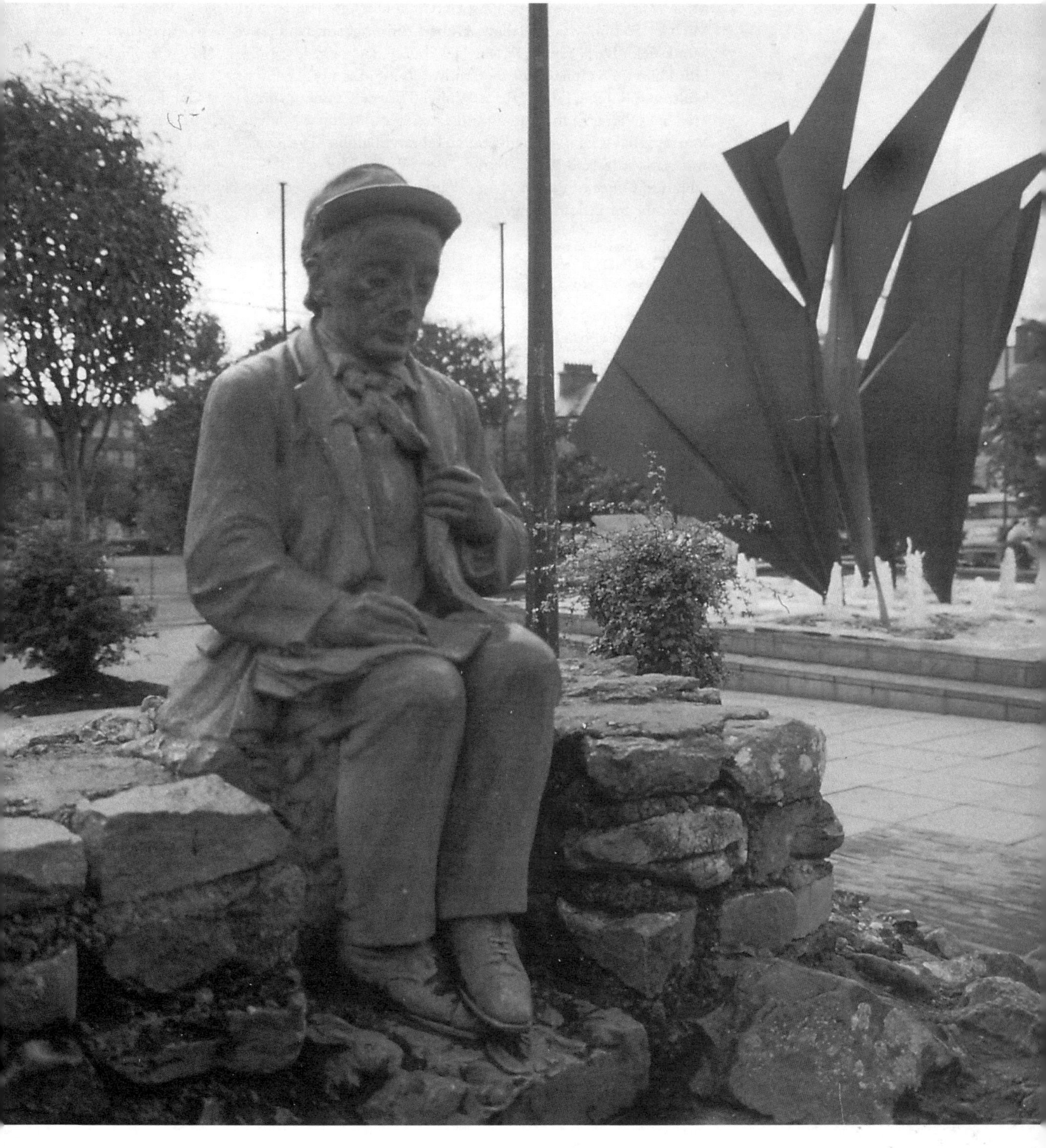

Pádraic Ó'Conaire statue in Eyre Square, Galway City

ACKNOWLEDGEMENTS

I would like to thank the following for their assistance in my preparation of this book: Mon Walsh, Dunmore; Peter Aspell; Ultan Macken; Pádraic Mullarkey, Barna; Fr Michael Tóibín, Mount Bellew; Hubert Birmingham, Dunmore; Cissie Connelly, Monksfield; Barry Flynn; Fr Michael Goaley, Glenamaddy; Bob Rooney, Craughwell; Eilís Dillon; Dympna Morgan; Trinity College Library, Dublin; Fr Patrick Gill, Milltown; Ritchie Foster; Brian White; Therese Cunningham; Gerry Connolly and Michael O'Hógain for reading and advising on the text; Michael Kelleher and Eileen Murray, Bray Library; The National Library, Dublin; Tynagh & District Development Association; Ireland West Tourism; Bord Fáilte; The staff of Galway, Tuam and Spiddal Libraries; Office of Public Works. Particular thanks to Geraldine Flynn and Noel Rowsome for proofreading.

First published 1995 by
WOLFHOUND PRESS Ltd
68 Mountjoy Square
Dublin 1

and Wolfhound Press (UK)
18 Coleswood Rd
Harpenden
Herts AL5 1EQ

British Library Cataloguing in Publication Data
A catalogue record for this book is available from the British Library.

ISBN 0 86327 428 5
Typesetting: Wolfhound Press
Cover design / Layout: Jan de Fouw
Cover photographs: Courtesy of Nutan
Printed in the Republic of Ireland by Colour Books, Dublin

Illustration: Bird's-eye view map, line drawings and photographs on pages 4, 70, 77, 79, 87, 90, 101, 109, 110 by Jan de Fouw. Maps on pages 10, 28, 34, 60, 89, 115, and illustration on page 25 by Jeanette Dunne. Photographs on pages 34, 38, 40, 47, 50, 53, 64, 76, 82, 99, 100, 103, 110, 112, 133, 136 courtesy of the author. Photographs on pages 1, 3, 12, 16, 18, 20, 29, 42, 43, 45, 52, 56 (right), 62, 63, 80, 88, 92, 113, 131, 132 by kind permission of Bord Fáilte. Photographs on pages 32, 56 (left), 70, 97, 98, 113, 117 by Michael Diggin. Photographs on pages 94, 119, 121, 129, 131, 139 courtesy of the Office of Public Works. Photographs on pages 127 courtesy of Michael Melia. Photograph on page 10 courtesy of the Galway Arts Festival. Photograph on page 36 courtesy of O'Brien Press. Photograph on page 65 (bottom) courtesy of The Irish Times. Photographs on page 65 by Grand National Pictures. Photograph on page 68 courtesy of Noel Pearson. Photograph on page 135 by kind permission of the Dublin Writers' Centre. Photograph on page 141 courtesy of Dunmore Heritage Committee. Photograph on page 143 by the Irish Peatland Conservation Council. Drawings on pages 73 and 80 from Hall's *The West and Connamara*, 1853
Colour illustration: As credited and photograph of musicians by Nutan.

The Book of Galway

CITY, TOWNS AND VILLAGES

Arthur Flynn

DESIGN AND ILLUSTRATION: JAN DE FOUW

WOLFHOUND PRESS

TO GARRETT FOR HIS HELP WITH THE RESEARCH.

LIST OF EVENTS

MARCH	Galway International Set Dancing Festival
	Irish Drama Festival, Cornamona.
APRIL	All-Ireland Confined Drama Finals, Glenamaddy.
	A T Cross Cúirt International Poetry Festival.
MAY	Currach Festival, Spiddal.
	Inishbofin Arts Festival.
	Bog Week, Letterfrack.
JUNE	Salmon and Lobster Festival, Roundstone.
	Sheep and Wool Festival, Leenane.
	Nature and Archaeology Weekend, Cleggan.
JULY	Galway Races, Ballybrit.
	Galway Arts Festival.
	Film Fleadh
	Salthill Festival
	Irish Showjumping Championships, Salthill.
	Kiltartan Hedge School, Gort.
	Ballyconneely Pony Show.
	Féile Mhic Dara, Carna.
	Loughrea Horse Show.
	The Shawl Festival, Oranmore.
	Roundstone Regatta.
	Queen of Connemara Festival, Oughterard.
	Portumna Summer Festival.
AUGUST	Gort Autumn Festival.
	Athenry Festival.
	Cruinniú na mBád, Kinvara.
	Annual Connemara Pony Show, Clifden.
	Dunmore Heritage Symposium.
SEPTEMBER	Galway International Oyster Festival.
	Clarinbridge Oyster Festival.
	Clifden Community Arts Week.
	Country Blues Festival, Clifden.
OCTOBER	Cultural Festival, Galway City.
	Ballinasloe International October Fair.
	October Horse Fair, Maam Cross.
DECEMBER	Woodford Mummers Féile.

Previous page: Eyre Square, Galway City (Brian Lynch, Bord Fáilte)

Contents

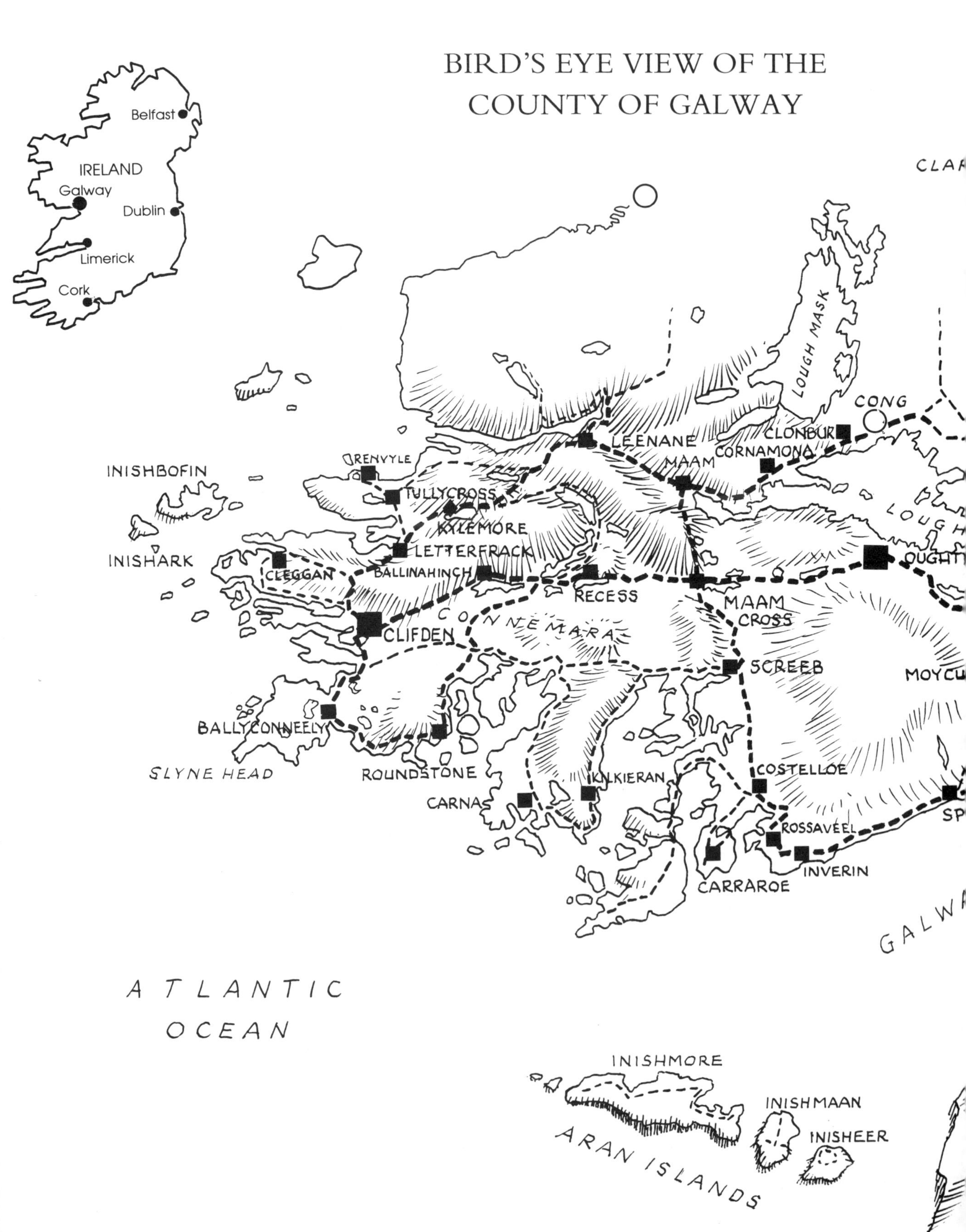
BIRD'S EYE VIEW OF THE
COUNTY OF GALWAY
Belfast
IRELAND
Galway
Dublin
Limerick
Cork
LOUGH MASK
CONG
CLONBUR
LEENANE
CORNAMONA
MAAM
RENVYLE
INISHBOFIN
TULLYCROSS
KYLEMORE
LETTERFRACK
INISHARK
CLEGGAN
BALLINAHINCH
RECESS
MAAM CROSS
CONNEMARA
CLIFDEN
SCREEB
BALLYCONNEELY
SLYNE HEAD
ROUNDSTONE
KILKIERAN
COSTELLOE
CARNA
ROSSAVEEL
INVERIN
CARRAROE
ATLANTIC
OCEAN
INISHMORE
INISHMAAN
INISHEER
ARAN ISLANDS

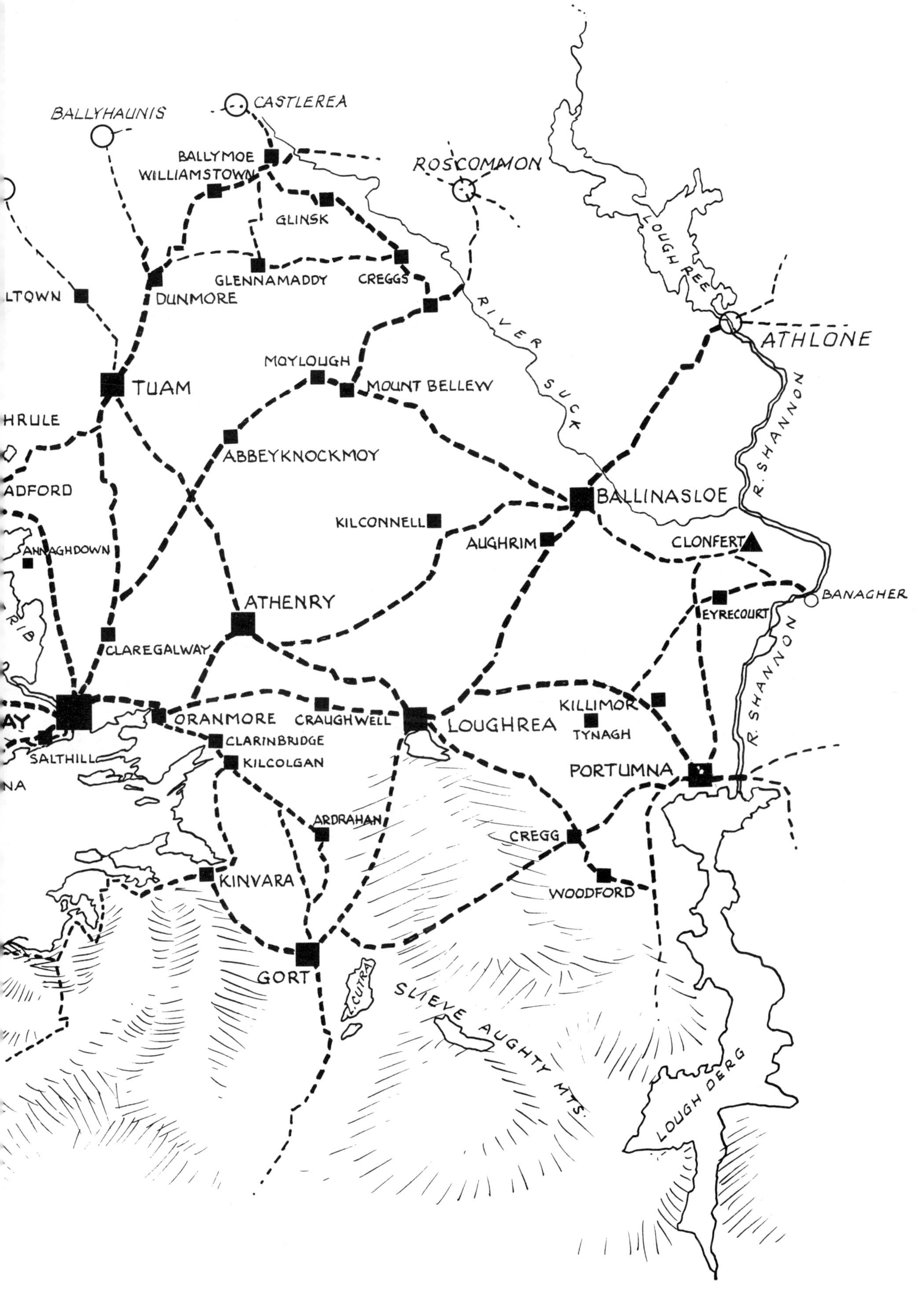

BALLYHAUNIS
CASTLEREA
BALLYMOE
WILLIAMSTOWN
GLINSK
ROSCOMMON
LOUGH REE
LTOWN
DUNMORE
GLENNAMADDY
CREGGS
RIVER SUCK
ATHLONE
MOYLOUGH
MOUNT BELLEW
TUAM
HRULE
R. SHANNON
ABBEYKNOCKMOY
ADFORD
BALLINASLOE
KILCONNELL
AUGHRIM
CLONFERT
ANNAGHDOWN
BANAGHER
ATHENRY
EYRECOURT
CLAREGALWAY
R. SHANNON
ORANMORE
CRAUGHWELL
LOUGHREA
KILLIMOR
TYNAGH
AY
CLARINBRIDGE
SALTHILL
KILCOLGAN
PORTUMNA
NA
ARDRAHAN
CREGG
KINVARA
WOODFORD
GORT
L. CUTRA
SLIEVE AUGHTY MTS.
LOUGH DERG

A Brief History of Ireland

At the end of the ice age, Mesolithic man came to Ireland, and traces of Mesolithic culture have been found along the Connemara coast. The Neolithic, or later stone age, culture began in Ireland around 6,500 years ago, leaving passage graves such as Newgrange in the Boyne valley. Stone Age people first arrived on Galway's isolated coastline over 5,000 years ago. Two thousand years later, bronze age man was to leave mine workings, traces of houses and fields, assembly places, copper and bronze tools and weapons, rock carvings and great wedge tombs scattered across Ireland. Dating from about 500 BC old roads, field systems, stone and promontory forts and ring, or earthen, forts can be seen (the most spectacular promontory fort in Ireland is Dún Aonghasa on the Aran Islands), and there remains an extraordinary body of Irish legends from this period that became the basis of much of early Irish literature for the next 2,000 years.

Christianity came to Galway in the fifth century AD, and many sites date from the following centuries - monasteries, inscribed crosses, tombstones, and island sites. St Edna founded a famous monastery on the Aran Islands in about 490. From around 800, Christian monastries became a focal point for those seeking refuge from Viking invaders. During the Viking wars powerful provincial kingdoms grew up in Ireland and these kingdoms waged continuous war against each other for the high-kingship of Ireland. Connacht was ruled by the O'Connors and for a long time it was the most powerful of the provincial kingdoms. The O'Connors made Tuam and Galway their capitals.

In 1170, the Normans came to Ireland under Strongbow – the beginning of an English military presence. They quickly overran most of the island, and assimilitated with the native Gaels. By the thirteenth century, the anglo-Norman had established strongholds throughout Ireland. Much of the lands of Galway were granted to the de Burgo family and they also took control of Galway city.

The thirteenth and fourteenth centuries saw constant disturbance in Galway, as the O'Connors and the O'Donnells fought against the Normans. In 1316 the Battle of Athenry gave victory to the de Burgos over the O'Connor clan. The fourteenth century was a period of in-fighting between the de Burgo family and the Albanachs and these two families dominate the history of this period.

By the time Henry VIII came to the throne, Ireland was ruled by chieftains who owed nominal allegiance to England. His daughter, Queen Elizabeth I, was to enforce that allegiance in wars that raged across the country. The city of Galway in the time of Henry VIII and Elizabeth I had paved streets, a large hospital, city walls and a quay. It was a royal city and was granted a charter from the king.

In 1649, Oliver Cromwell led a powerful force to subdue Ireland. The period of fighting which followed, known as the Cromwellian era, ended the political and economic power of the great Gaelic families and established a Protestant asendancy.

At the end of the seventeenth century, a series of harsh laws, known as the Penal Laws were in force against Catholics (who formed the majority of the population) prohibiting them from holding any office of state, voting, buying or holding a long lease on land, etc. By the late eighteenth century, barely 5% of land remained in Catholic hands. It was not until 1829 that Catholic Emancipation of Ireland was won with the repeal of these laws.

In the 1840s, the potato crop failed all over Ireland, resulting in the Great Irish Famine. The combination of disease, starvation and the heavy emigration that followed drastically reduced Ireland's population. By 1850, when the worst of the famine was over, Ireland had lost more than two million of her population of eight million.

In modern times Ireland saw more upheaval, from the Fenian rebellions of the nineteenth century (led by the Irish Republican Brotherhood – IRB – and the Irish Republican Army – IRA, not to be confused with the modern-day terrorist IRA who bear the same name), to the 1916 Rising centred on Dublin's General Post Office, the arrival of the famous Black and Tan military force from Britain, through the War of Independence (1919-21) ending with the Anglo-Irish Treaty of 1921 that established a 26-county republic, and the bitterly divisive Civil War (1922-23) between Pro- and Anti-Treaty forces which left its mark on Irish and Galway politics for the next half-century.

In the latter half of the twentieth century, Galway reflects all that is best in a changing modern Ireland – a fine linkage of traditional culture, thriving and co-existing in a modern context with booming tourist and other successful local businesses reaching international markets.

Preface

County Galway, the second largest county in Ireland, is situated mid-way along the west coast, in the province of Connacht. The county extends from Killary Harbour in the north, across the Maamturk Mountains to Lough Corrib, and Galway Bay. On the eastern side it borders County Roscommon and extends southwards to the Burren and Lough Derg. The Atlantic Ocean forms its western boundary.

This large county, officially established in the sixteenth century, is divided into two contrasting regions by the great expanse of Lough Corrib. East of the lake is a fertile limestone plain, extending to the Galway-Roscommon border and the River Shannon. The area of prime interest to tourists lies mainly west of Lough Corrib, a region of magnificent mountain, lake and coastal scenery. The Twelve Bens, a striking range of conical peaks interspersed with deep lake-filled valleys, are the chief mountain feature. Southwards, great tracts of lake-dotted bogland stretch down to the indented rocky coast.

Galway, made famous in song by Bing Crosby, offers a variation of landscape, scenery, traditional customs and historical sites. Galway city, with its coastal suburb of Salthill, is one of the country's most important tourist centres and the fastest developing city in Europe. It is also the gateway to the picturesque areas of the country, and to the western Gaeltacht (including the Aran Islands), where Irish is the everyday language of the people. Another major attraction for tourists is the excellent salmon and trout fishing in the rivers and lakes.

In the book I have divided the county into several broad areas:

1. *Galway City and its environs*.
2. *The Aran Islands*.
3. *South Connemara:* extending from Barna to Carna to Maam Cross and back via Oughterard to Galway.
4. *North Connemara:* extending from Maam Cross to Leenane, around the coast to Clifden and from Roundstone to Recess.
5. *South Galway*: beginning at Oranmore and including such attractions as Thoor Ballylee, Coole Estate and Clonfert and on to Portumna.
6. *East Galway*: covers many historic centres from Claregalway and Annaghdown to Tuam and Glenamaddy.

In each section I give a short history of every town and village. In addition I offer my personal choice of places worth visiting, from historic sites to beaches to good fishing locations. I also recommend pubs, coffee shops, restaurants, hotels, hostels and venues providing traditional music.

The attractions of County Galway for me are many: the uncluttered roads of south and east Galway; the unspoilt mountains, beaches, rivers and lakes of Connemara; the lilt of an impromptu music session around a turf fire; the mixed emotions of fear and elation, travelling by currach, in a choppy sea, from Inishmaan to Inishmore; watching a screening of *Man of Aran* (1932/4) with the people whose life it portrays; and the spectacular Connemara National Park, stretching from Letterfrack to the heart of the Twelve Bens Mountain range.

The largest and most prosperous towns in County Galway are Clifden, Tuam, Ballinasloe, Gort and Loughrea. Many prominent personalities have had connections with the county including Pádraig Pearse, 'Lord Haw Haw', Lady Gregory, W B Yeats, Kate O'Brien, Nora Barnacle, Walter Macken, Pádraic Ó'Conaire, Liam O'Flaherty, Orson Welles, John Huston and Eilís Dillon.

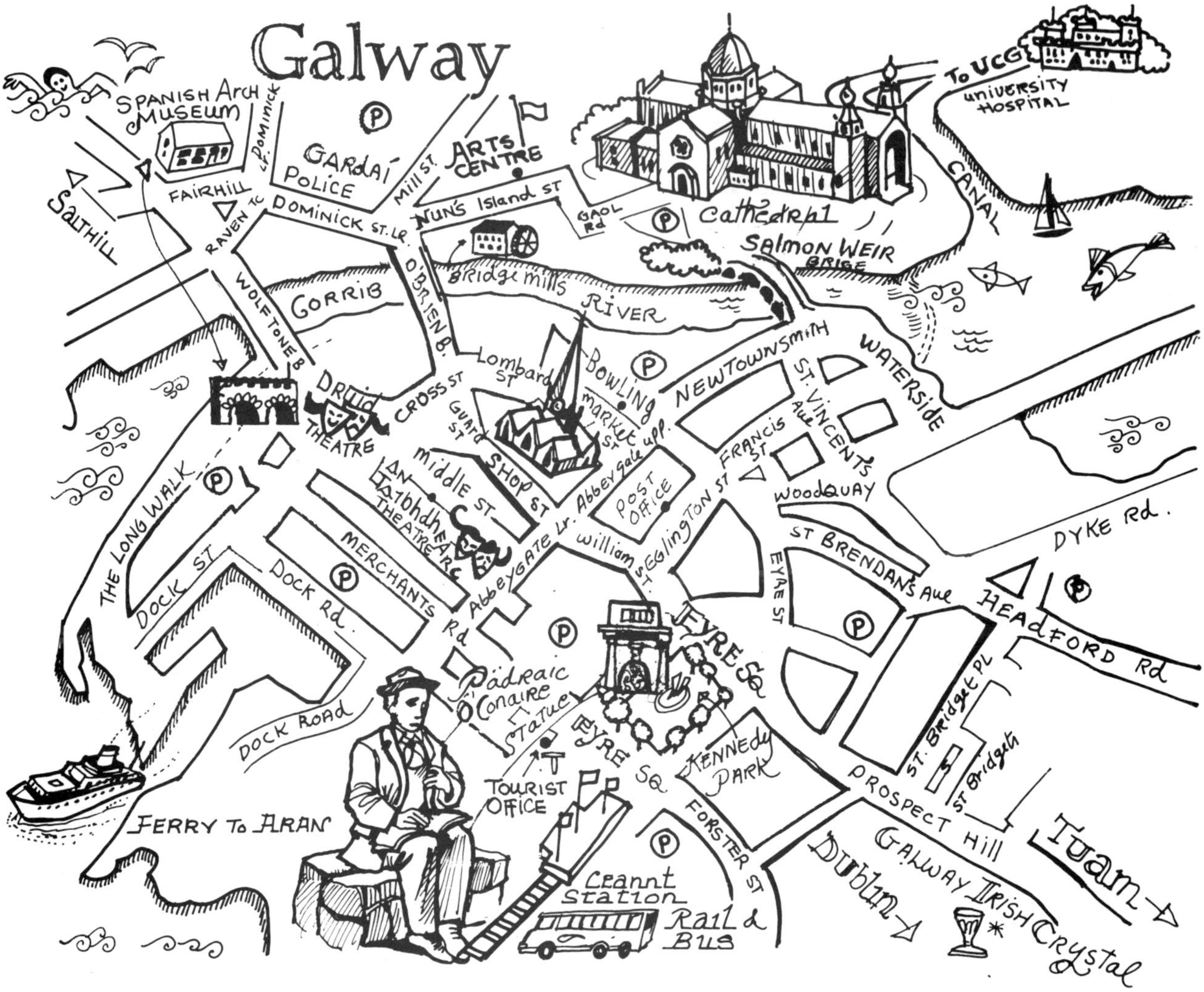

Galway

SPANISH ARCH MUSEUM
DOMINICK LR.
GARDAÍ POLICE
MILL ST.
ARTS CENTRE
NUN'S Island ST
GAOL Rd
Cathedral
To UCG
UNIVERSITY HOSPITAL
CANAL
SALTHILL
FAIRHILL
RAVEN TC
DOMINICK ST. LR.
SALMON WEIR BRIDGE
BRIDGE MILLS
O'BRIEN B.
CORRIB RIVER
WOLFTONE B
Lombard ST
BOWLING
NEWTOWNSMITH
WATERSIDE
ST. VINCENTS AVE
DRUID THEATRE
CROSS ST
GUARD ST
market ST
Abbeygate upp.
FRANCIS ST
middle ST.
SHOP ST
POST OFFICE
EGLINGTON ST
WOODQUAY
AN TAIBHDHEARC THEATRE
THE LONG WALK
william ST.
ST BRENDANS AVE
DYKE Rd.
DOCK ST
DOCK Rd.
MERCHANTS Rd
Abbeygate Lr.
EYRE ST
HEADFORD Rd
EYRE SQ
Pádraic Conaire Statue
DOCK ROAD
KENNEDY PARK
ST. BRIDGETS PL
ST BRIDGETS
TOURIST OFFICE
EYRE SQ.
PROSPECT HILL
FERRY TO ARAN
FORSTER ST
GALWAY IRISH CRYSTAL
Ceannt Station
Rail & Bus
Dublin
Tuam

Galway City

HISTORY

Galway city, the principal town of Connacht, is situated at the estuary of the River Corrib. There is a belief that the name Galway originated from a colony of Gauls who were thought to have settled there. Prior to the reign of King Henry II, Galway was little more than a small fishing village, protected by a fortress, known as Baile na Sruthán (The Town of the Little Streams). Another source indicates that the English settlement became known as Ballinagall or Gaillibh (The Foreigner's Town). The *Annals of the Four Masters* suggest that Galway derived its name from the river in which Gaillimh, daughter of Breasil, a pre-Celtic King, was drowned. Camden believed that the name originated from the Gallaeci of Spain, a country which traded with Galway. In some early documents the town is referred to as 'near Athenry'.

The *Annals of the Four Masters* stated that in 927 the Vikings made their way up the River Corrib and raided small settlements. Up to the twelfth century Galway was no more than a village of the O'Flaherty clan. In 1124 Turlough O'Connor, King of Connacht, built the wooden castle of Bun Gaillimhe. A small community developed around the castle. In 1132 Conor O'Brien, King of Munster, sent a force by sea, under Cormac McCarthy, to capture and destroy the castle. They killed all the members of the garrison, including Conor O'Flaherty. The castle was rebuilt; but in 1149 it was destroyed again, by Turlough O'Brien. Four years later the ships from the port, which were called 'the Galway Dune', took part in an expedition led by Roderic O'Connor against O'Loughlin, Prince of Tyrone, and defeated him.

GALWAY - BROWNE'S GATEWAY

In 1230 when the Anglo-Normans invaded Connacht, Galway became a strategic location for them with its coastal position and control of the river crossing. Galway then only consisted of a few dozen families and fishermen, under the protection of the O'Flahertys. Hugh O'Flaherty fortified the castle and resisted several onslaughts by Richard de Burgo. De Burgo finally succeeded in capturing the territory of the O'Flahertys and the O'Hallorans. The Anglo-Normans built a stronghold, fortified by a castle beside the river. Despite frequent attacks by the O'Flahertys the de Burgos held firm and defended the castle and territory. In 1270 the de Burgos received a grant of murage to finance the building of a city wall. Under their control the status of the town increased significantly and population and trade grew. By the end of the thirteenth century, Welsh and English families were encouraged to settle in the area to restrain the native O'Flahertys and the other dispossessed clans.

Facing page: Macnas, theatrical Galway troup

In 1296 Sir William Leigh de Burgh founded the Franciscan Friary on St Stephen's Island, outside the north gate. It became the main burial place for leading families in the district. In 1312 the Great Gates and extra walls were added by Nicholas Lynch, the Provost Marshall. In the twelfth century and later in 1498 efforts were made to construct an artificial cutting linking Lough Corrib with the sea at Galway Bay.

From 1330 with the decline of the British Crown's control in Connacht and the inter-marriage of the Anglo-Normans with the native Irish, the Galway settlement became isolated. In 1333 William de Burgo, the Brown Earl, was murdered. His baby daughter, Elizabeth, became heir to his estate but his territory in Connacht was seized and the conflict only concluded when Edmund a son of Richard de Burgo, The Red Earl of Ulster, was captured by Éamonn Albanach and drowned in Lough Mask. William Albanach took over the lands in County Galway and became mayor of Galway.

In a document of 1376 Galway is not mentioned in a list of Irish cities and main towns. By 1388 William Burke was appointed master of Galway. On 8 November 1396 a new perpetual murage charter was granted to the inhabitants by King Richard II. In 1402 this charter was confirmed by King Henry IV who also granted it a licence to coin money. On 28 August 1464 a further charter was granted to the town, which gave it power to elect a mayor and a bailiff of its own and contained a clause that 'neither the Lord Mac William of Clanrickard, nor his heirs, should settle anything in the town without permission.'

By the fifteenth century Galway had established strong trading links with France, Spain and Portugal. The main exports from Galway were linen, wool, leather, farm produce and fish. One of the main imports from Spain was wine. The area around the Spanish Arch leading to Spanish Parade was a favourite promenade of the Spanish merchants and their families. In 1473 a disastrous fire destroyed many of Galway's buildings but this was quickly followed by the rebuilding of the city.

The clergy of Galway resented the fact that they were controlled by the Archbishop of Tuam who would allocate priests to the parish. In 1484 a wardenship of Galway was established which was confirmed by the Bull of Pope Innocent VIII the following year. It decreed a separate ecclesiastical jurisdiction for Galway under a warden and eight vicars. This Wardenship, which was continued by the Established Church in the Protestant tradition after the Reformation, was not discontinued until 1840. In 1488 the Dominican Friary was founded in Galway. In the seventeenth century the building was destroyed by fire but was later rebuilt. Among the most notable architectural features are stained glass windows by Michael Healy.

In 1493 Walter Lynch, son of James Lynch FitzStephen, travelled to Spain as master of one of his father's ships. The son, wild and undisciplined, ran up substantial debts and, during a struggle, he threw a Spaniard overboard. He returned to Galway, reformed his ways and prepared to marry, but, on his death bed, a fellow sailor and accomplice, confessed to the murder. Acting as Chief Magistrate of Galway, James Lynch FitzStephen was forced to try his own son, and sentence him to death. The Lynch clan rose in an attempt to rescue the son, and avert a disgrace to the family. Lynch took his son to his own house and hanged him from one of the windows, under which was carved a skull and crossbones to mark the public abhorrence of the tragic event. The broken-hearted father then retired into seclusion. A play entitled, *The Warden of Galway*, was written about the tragedy.

From the beginning of the sixteenth century there was large scale development in Galway. St Brigid's Hospital was founded for the poor of the town and each burgess was obliged to send a maid servant to collect alms every Sunday for its support. In 1543 the charitable institute was opened when the 'sweating sickness' broke out, resulting in wide scale fatalities. In 1578 a charter of Elizabeth I granted power to the Corporation to build a jail. The following year the city received a garrison but as there was no barracks, the troops were stationed in a house.

With so many vessels using the port it was inevitable that tragedies would occur. In 1560 at Cuan an Fhir Mhóir, one hundred men died in a ship wreck. In 1588 one of the ships of the ill-fated Spanish Armada was wrecked in Galway Bay and up to seventy of the crew were drowned. Two hundred Spaniards who survived were butchered by order of Lord Deputy Sir William Fitzwilliam.

In 1580 Mayor Dominick Lynch established a Free School in Galway. In 1599 the convent of St Brigid, near Galway, was burned by Hugh Ruadh O'Donnell, Prince of Tyrconnell. In August 1602 the fortification of Galway was complete and a fort was erected. On 14 June 1613 a patent was granted for a fair in Galway. This was known as the Claddagh Fair and was held at Fair Hill or at St Dominick's Abbey on 24 August and the two days following. Two years later King James I suppressed the Free School but it was later revived. The school produced some famous headmasters including Alexander Lynch and John Lynch, author of 'Cambrenis Eversus.' By 1627 there were so many scholars converging on Galway that the Corporation ordered foreigners and beggars to be whipped out of the town. Following the Cromwellian campaign of 1652 the school closed.

In 1641 a Corporation Charter guaranteed privileges and provided for liberty to trade. All prisoners, natives or inhabitants of Galway or Aran, were to be released without ransom and all merchandise confiscated at sea was to be returned. This did not happen and Galway was to experience a turbulent period from 1641 to the 1650s. In 1651 Sir Charles

Coote, the Cromwellian General commenced a nine month land-and-sea blockade of Galway which ended with the surrender of the town on 5 April 1652. Starvation forced the Irish to capitulate. Galway was the last Irish town to hold out against Cromwell's forces.

'The Tribes of Galway' was a term first used by Cromwell's forces, referring to the co-operation between the native Irish and the Anglo-Irish. 'The Tribes' consisted of fourteen ruling families of Galway. Among the most distinguished of these tribes was the Lynch family, which had a major influence on the town providing eighty-four mayors between 1485 and 1654. The other tribes were: Athy, Blake, Bodkin, Browne, D'Arcy, Deane, Font, French, Joyce, Kirwan, Martin, Morris and Skerret.

In a further Charter of August 1676, the King granted that 'the town of Galway should, at all times, for ever thereafter, be one entire and one free borough of itself, to be known by the name of the town and borough of Galway.' One difficulty in Galway was that there was only one bridge over the River Corrib and the streets were too narrow to move cattle from one side to the other. The solution to the problem was to hold fairs on the east and west side of the town. The western location was beside the Dominican Friary and the eastern fair was held at the square plot, now Eyre Square.

In 1689 the Governor ordered the removal of Protestant inhabitants to the western suburbs for better security in the town. On 24 March 1701 Queen Anne came to the throne and ordered the commissioning of three companies of foot soldiers, consisting of 250 men raised in the town and liberties of Galway. In 1715 troops occupied the convents following the dispersion of the nuns. In 1734 the castle or upper citadel barracks was built near William's Gate. Over a decade later the Shambles Barracks was built to accommodate ten companies. A public infirmary was erected in a small building at Wood Quay and later moved to a spacious house in Abbeygate Street. Finally a new infirmary was built which could accommodate up to 800 people.

In September 1776 a travel writer gave the following account of Galway: 'The poor people near Galway are very industrious in buying the sullage of the streets of that town; they give 3*d* for a horse load of two baskets, and carry it three miles.'

At the start of the nineteenth century there was much improvement at several levels: educational, maritime and commercial. Galway was one of the locations in Ireland, chosen by Erasmus Smith, the adventurer, for his schools which became known as the Erasmus Smith Free Schools. It opened in August 1815. In 1845 a Bill was introduced in Parliament by Sir Robert Peel, who established Ireland's first police force (which became known as The Peelers), to set up the Queen's Colleges University of Ireland comprising of colleges in Belfast, Cork and

Galway. In 1846 the foundations of Queen's University, Galway were laid. The college was built in a Tudor style design by Joseph B Keane, based on the Cambridge College concept. The college opened on 30 October 1849 with an initial intake of sixty-eight students. It is now known as University College, Galway.

In 1834 the writer Maria Edgeworth visited the city and gave the following description: 'Next day to Galway and still it was fine weather, and right for the open carriage, and we thought it would always be so. Galway wet or dry, and it was wet when I saw it, is the dirtiest town I ever saw and the most desolate and idle-looking. He (Dr Veitch, a friend of the Edgeworth family) walked with us all over Galway, and showed us all that was worth seeing, from the new quay projecting, and the new green Connemara marble-cutters' workshop, to the old Spanish houses with projecting roofs and piazza walks beneath; and wading through seas of yellow mud thick as stirabout, we went to see archways that had stood centuries, and above all to the old mayoralty house of that mayor of Galway who hung his own son.'

Under an Act of 1836, a chairman and twenty-four commissioners were elected to administer the city. In 1853 £40,000 was allocated to build new streets and to supply every house with water. A grant was made to improve the harbour and raise it to the standard of a transatlantic station. The Galway Packet line commenced operation from the harbour. A new dock was constructed which allowed for the docking of vessels of fourteen foot draught. The Bianconi coach service ran from Galway to Clifden. Trade in the region was flourishing and a gas company was established to light the town. Soon the town was extending into the suburbs. The trades and industries included distilleries, breweries, a paper mill and a foundry. Before the famine of 1847 there were twenty-five mills employed in the manufacture of flour.

Following the great famine of 1847, hundreds of the poor and desolate travelled from all over the country to Galway harbour to take the emigration boats to America. Some of the gloom and depression was lifted with the boost to commerce and tourism brought about by the extension of the railway line from Dublin to Galway. The line, run by the Midland Great Western Railway, opened to the public on 1 August 1851.

On 17 August 1869 the first meeting of the famous Galway Races was held at Ballybrit Racecourse. Forty thousand people attended the meeting and a campsite was opened at Eyre Square to accommodate the crowd.

February 1886 is an important date in the political history of Galway, as Charles Stewart Parnell imposed Captain William O'Shea on the electorate of the city. Parnell had to travel to Galway to prevent a mutiny of his party and to insist on O'Shea's candidacy.

In 1890 the British Government established The Congested Districts Board to help promote small industries in the more impoverished areas, particularly in the west of Ireland. In 1896, the Board launched the first regular steamer service between Galway and the Aran Islands. It also encouraged the development of sea fishing and related industries. In 1893 Conradh na Gaeilge (The Gaelic League) began a revival of Irish culture with a particular emphasis on the Irish language. Five years later Galway County Council was established. Galway was foremost in the language revival and in 1929 Galway University was chosen as a centre of bilingual higher education. Around this period Taibhdhearc na Gaillimhe, a theatre devoted entirely to plays in the Irish language, was opened. In 1937 Galway Corporation and the office of Mayor were granted full statutory recognition. The county's efforts towards the revival of the language were rewarded in 1969 when Gaeltarra Eireann (established to promote industries in the Gaeltacht) decentralised its headquarters from Dublin to Furbo, seven miles from Galway. In 1980 it in turn was replaced by Udarás na Gaeltachta (a development authority).

THE CLADDAGH

The Claddagh on the west bank of the River Corrib was the original Irish centre of the English city of Galway, and was situated outside the city walls. Claddagh is an anglicised Irish word meaning 'A Flat Stoney Shore'. It is believed that the Claddagh pre-dated Galway city and that the inhabitants who lived outside the city walls were descendants of Gaelic families and spoke Irish. The area consisted of a collection of small, narrow, cobble-stoned streets with thatched mud cabins. The people from the area had their own customs and rituals and were inclined to marry within their own community. At one stage the area had a population of 8,000.

The Claddagh ring dates from the seventeenth century when one of the Joyce family returned from Algeria as a goldsmith and began to practise his trade in the Claddagh. The ring once handmade by Galway goldsmiths was for a long period the wedding ring of much of Connemara and the Aran Islands. The ring depicts a heart and two hands clasped in friendship and is now known worldwide.

The Claddagh fishermen claimed the exclusive right of fishing in Galway Bay. About 150 Claddagh sail boats were employed in fishing and also about 100 rowing boats which were used mainly for catching herring. There was a tradition that when strange boats fished in Galway Bay they were protected by a gun brig. When the brig had departed, the Claddagh fishermen would resume their dominance over the bay.

The people of the Claddagh elected their own mayor, sheriff and other officers on St John's Day and they would then march through the district in procession. The mayor's boat was distinguishable by a white sail and flag and when the fishing season began the fleet assembled and, following a signal, the nets were cast and drawn simultaneously, after which every boat could fish alone. Later there was a King of the Claddagh, who governed the area and resolved disputes and feuds. The King had the title 'Admiral of Galway Bay' and his boat had also got a white sail replacing the black and brown sails of the other fishing boats from the Claddagh. Eoin Concannon, the last King of the Claddagh, died in 1954 aged ninety. The Annual Blessing of the sea which took place at the beginning of the herring season was an impressive ceremony. The fleet of fishing boats moved out into the bay, headed by a vessel which was specially decorated for the occasion. This vessel carried priests from the Dominican Church, and acolytes bearing lighted tapers. On reaching the appointed spot, the sails were lowered and the blessing of the bay commenced.

Walter Macken, the author who was born in St Joseph's Avenue, Galway, set one of his best known books, *Rain on the Wind*, in the Claddagh.

In 1934 the cottages of the Claddagh were declared unhealthy and the entire district, with the exception of the Dominican Church, was demolished and replaced by more conventional dwellings.

ARTISTIC and LITERARY TRADITION

Galway has always been proud of its strong literary and artistic tradition which dates from the days of Lady Gregory and the Irish literary revival to today when many writers, poets, film makers and playwrights have made the city their base.

A century and a half before the Taibhdhearc, at the end of the eighteenth century, Richard Martin opened a small theatre in Kirwan's Lane. A building three doors from the Taibhdhearc in Middle Street was once the Racquet Court Theatre where many touring companies performed dramas and musicals. John McCormack played there early in his career.

Taibhdhearc na Gaillimhe, the only theatre in Ireland devoted entirely to plays in the Irish language opened in September 1928 with Micheál Mac Liammóir's production of *Diarmuid agus Gráinne*. Walter Macken worked at the theatre between 1939-47 as Manager/Actor and produced seventy-seven plays in Irish. Macken was born in Galway in 1915 and became a prolific writer, writing both novels and plays. His most successful plays were *Mungo's Mansion* and *Home Is the Hero*. His best known books are *Rain in the Wind* (for his study of Claddagh fishermen) and his topical trilogy *Seek the Fair Land* about Cromwellian Ireland, *The Silent People* about the Famine years of the nineteenth

Nora Barnacle's House, (Bord Fáilte)

century, and *The Scorching Wind* about the Troubles of the twentieth century. Siobhán McKenna, the actress, was another distinguished figure to be associated with the Taibhdhearc. She was born in Belfast in 1923 and studied at University College, Galway. Her first stage appearance was at the theatre when she translated George Bernard Shaw's *St Joan* into Irish and played the title role.

Another important venue in Galway is the Druid Theatre in Chapel Lane, which has been a phenomenal success in recent years. The company, founded in 1975, by a group from the university, headed by Garry Hynes and Mick Lally, has achieved a national and international reputation for its revival of Anglo-Irish productions and plays by new playwrights. Two of their most notable productions were John Millington Synge's *Playboy of the Western World* and Tom Murphy's *Bailegangaire*. The company stages lunchtime and evening performances. A recent addition to the theatrical scene in Galway is the Punchbag Theatre Company. Along with the Arts Festival, the A T Cross Cúirt Festival of Literature held each April attracts some of the finest poets and novelists writing today. One of the most popular events during the year is the Music for Galway Concert Season which presents orchestral concerts, chamber music and traditional music at various venues.

Nora Barnacle, who became James Joyce's wife, was born in 8 Bowling Green on 21 March 1884. Nora met Joyce while she worked in Finn's Hotel in Dublin. Their first date was on 16 June 1904, which has become known as Bloomsday and was the date on which his masterpiece *Ulysses* was set. James Joyce came to Galway numerous times between 1909 and 1912 to visit his in-laws. The Joyces later moved to Trieste. The house in Bowling Green is now open to the public and regular literary evenings are held there. A memorial plaque was unveiled on the building in 1982 to mark the centenary of Joyce's birth.

Nora Barnacle

Pádraic Ó Conaire, who was a leading figure in the literary revival in Ireland, was born in Galway in 1882. He later moved to London but, following the death of his parents, returned to Rosmuc, in County Galway, and continued to write short stories in Irish.

The film director, Joe Comerford made the critically acclaimed film, *Reefer and the Model*, based in Galway. Lelia Doolan, who served as producer on the film was appointed Chairperson of the newly formed Film Board in 1993. The Film Board is now centred in Galway. Following the General Election of November 1992, Michael D. Higgins, the Labour TD for Galway was appointed the first Minister for the Arts, Culture and the Gaeltacht.

The writer Eilís Dillon was born in Galway in 1920 and became a versatile writer, producing novels, plays and children's books. Amongst her best known works are *Across the Bitter Sea, The Lost Island, Inside Ireland , The Singing Cave, The Island of Ghosts* and *The Bitter Glass*. Other writers associated with Galway are Rita Ann Higgins, poet; John Arden, playwright and novelist and Margaretta D'Arcy, playwright.

GALWAY TODAY

Over the past two decades Galway has been transformed into a cosmopolitan centre, pulsating with atmosphere and life. The developers of the recent upsurge of urban renewal in the city have retained the best of the old façades and incorporated new buildings into the structures. Several derelict sites have been converted into modern shopping centres and hotels. Two good examples are the Eyre Square Shopping Centre and the Spanish Arch Project with the new Jury's Inn and tasteful apartment blocks.

Since the late 1970s locals and foreigners have seen the potential in the developing city and have begun opening medium priced restaurants, craft shops and galleries. Their foresight is now paying dividends as Galway is firmly established as a popular holiday centre. During the summer months the population of over 50,000 is swollen considerably. With the University and Regional College and opportunities in business and industry, the city attracts many young people who make their presence felt on the streets, in the pubs, discos and shops.

The people of Galway city and its environs have long realised the potential of tourism and provide top standards in hotels, restaurants, pubs and guesthouses. The city is renowned for its unique series of Festivals. Cúirt International Poetry Festival in April attracts leading poets from home and abroad. The month of July offers a host of festivals including the Galway Races, one of the social and sporting highlights of the year, the Film Fleadh, the Salthill Festival and of course the Galway Arts Festival, which has become one of the foremost events in the country. One of the most popular features of this festival is the appearance of Macnas, with larger than life characters in unusual costumes. The Galway Oyster Festival in September also attracts large crowds.

Music and merry-making are not confined to festival time but is a year round phenomenon with buskers liberally scattered around the streets. Pubs and traditional music are an integral part of city life and many licensed premises provide night time sessions. A favourite venue for young people is The Quays pub. Galway can be proud of the many musicians who have emerged from its environs, headed by the rock group, The Stunning, the fine musicians of Dé Dannan and solo singers such as Dolores Keane and Mary Coughlan.

Galway abounds with bookshops which include Easons, and Kennys, one of the best known bookshops and art galleries in the country. There are other art galleries at the Grainstore, the Arts Centre and the Geoghegan Gallery.

The city is compact enough to be walked and viewed at a leisurely pace. A popular area for strollers is around Cross Street/Quay Street with pubs, small attractive shops and medium priced restaurants.

Those wishing to experience a true flavour of the city should join one of the walking tours. They come under three headings: Medieval, Maritime and Literary and they take place daily from the Tourist Office. Travellers wishing to proceed on their own should buy a copy of *A Tourist Trail of Old Galway*. A stroll along stretches of the River Corrib, particularly when it is in flood, is to be recommended. A must for all visitors during the spawning season is to watch the shoals of salmon leaping, close to the Salmon Weir Bridge. Another interesting walk is around the docks area and the very energetic should walk over Wolfe Tone Bridge, turn left and continue along the coast road which will eventually link them to the Salthill promenade. The Saturday market outside St Nicholas's Church is well worth a browse. Royal Tara China welcomes visitors to the showrooms and for factory tours.

GALWAY LANDMARKS

Galway Catholic Cathedral: The cathedral was built on the west bank of the River Corrib between 1959-69 on the site of the former jail. The building, designed by John J Robinson, was dedicated to Our Lady Assumed into Heaven and St Nicholas and was officially opened in August 1965 by Cardinal Cushing of Boston. The cruciform interior, replete with greenish-grey limestone and Connemara marble, can seat 2000 people. You will also find a trio of stained glass windows depicting John F. Kennedy, Christ rising from the dead and Pádraig Pearse.

Eyre Square: The square in the centre of the city was originally an open space in front of the main gates. One of the best known features in the park is the statue of Pádraic Ó Conaire, the Galway writer, who wrote short stories in Irish in the 1920s. The statue was sculpted by Albert Power. At the western end there is a doorway from a mansion built by the Browne family in Abbeygate Street Lower in 1627. It was transferred to the Square in 1905. There is a statue of Liam Mellows, a Galway leader in the 1916 Rising. The two huge cannons were presented to the Connaught Rangers at the end of the Crimean War. The park now bears the name, John Fitzgerald Kennedy Memorial Park and there is a monument to commemorate the former President of the United States' visit in 1963, when he received the Freedom of the City. A recent addition to the park is the Quincentennial Fountain. At the eastern end stands the impressive bulk of the Great Southern Hotel.

St Nicholas's Church: Erected in 1320, enlarged in 1486, and modified a number of times between then and the nineteenth century, this Church of Ireland church has many interesting exhibits and tombs, dating back to the Middle Ages. Christopher Columbus is reputed to have prayed here in 1477, before setting forth on his voyage of discovery.

City Walls: Portions of the old city walls have been cleverly incorporated into the Eyre Square Centre.

Old Buildings: It is recommended to stroll around the streets and view the fine architecture of the old doorways, windows and traditional shop fronts. An architectural inventory is available.

Spanish Arch: The arch is situated in the south-western section of the old town. This was one of four arches, but did not form part of the city wall, a section of which can be seen nearby. The arch leads on to Spanish Parade, where, according to tradition, the Spanish merchants used to stroll in the evening. Adjacent to the arch is a museum.

Salmon Weir Bridge: In season dozens of salmon can be seen lying on the river bed or leaping as they head upriver to the spawning grounds in Lough Corrib.

Merchant House: There are many examples in the city centre of the old merchant houses constructed in the seventeenth and eighteenth centuries. They can be found chiefly in Shop Street, Saint Augustine St, Abbeygate St and Middle St.

Lynch's Castle: This castle, in Shop Street is now the Allied Irish Bank, and is believed to have been built during the reign of Henry VIII. The building is noted for its decorative coat of arms and carved stone work. In 1493 Mayor Lynch hanged his son, Walter, from one of the windows.

Franciscan Abbey: The abbey was built in Francis Street in 1836, on the site of a friary founded by the de Burgos in 1296.

Galway New Cemetery: Is worth a visit to view the graves of many distinguished people who had associations with the county including,

RECOMMENDED

Fat Freddy's Pizza Warehouse.

The Whole Hog Pizza Bar.

Bewleys.

GBC Restaurant.

Cobwebs.

Great Southern Hotel.

The Brasserie Restaurant.

Jurys Inn.

The Rolling Donut.

Sunflower Vegetarian Restaurant. River Run Gallery.

Western Tandoori.

Paddy's Bar (Music).

The Quays Pub (Music).

Burke's Pub.

Lísheen Bar.

Victoria Club.

Brennan's Yard Hotel.

Ardilaun House Hotel.

Victoria Hotel.

Corrib Great Southern Hotel.

Galway Ryan Hotel.

Imperial Hotel.

Grand Hotel Hostel.

Eyre House Restaurant.

Seventh Heaven Restaurant.

Shama Restaurant (Indian).

Hooker Jimmy's.

Galway Kart Racing.

Leisure Dome.

The Galway Bowl.

Galway Omniplex.

Galway City Gym.

Galway Lawn Tennis Club.

Galway Cycle Hire, Eyre Square.

RECOMMENDED

Punchbag Theatre.
Druid Theatre.
Tourist Office.
Nora Barnacle Museum.
Galway Arts Festival.
Galway Races.
Galway Oyster Festival.
AT Cross Cuirt International Poetry Festival.
International Pan Celtic Festival.

Pádraic Ó Conaire, the author; Lady Gregory, co-founder of the Abbey Theatre; Walter Macken, the author and playwright and William Joyce, known as 'Lord Haw-Haw' for his German broadcasts during the Second World War.

Galway Arts Centre: The centre, situated in Dominick Street, stages plays, poetry readings and art exhibitions.

Royal Tara: The visitors' centre and china showrooms are located in Mervue and visitors are welcome to view the craft factories and exhibits.

The Bridge Mills: The building, beside O'Brien's Bridge, dates to the late eighteenth century but was restored in 1988. It now houses a restaurant, gallery, language centre, pottery and antique shops.

Galway Irish Crystal: The factory is located on the Dublin Road and welcomes visitors for factory tours.

Courthouse: The building, close to the Salmon Weir Bridge, which now sadly has a shabby appearance, was built to a design by Richard Morrison in 1812.

St Mary's Catholic Church: This Dominican church is situated in the Claddagh, on the banks of the River Corrib. It is worth a visit to see the seventeenth century wooden statue of Our Lady of Galway.

Ballybrit Racecourse: This is the setting of the famous Galway Races held annually at the end of July. The first race meeting was held on 17 August 1869. In 1979 the racecourse was also the location of the Young People's Mass celebrated by Pope John Paul II during his historic visit to Galway. A memorial now stands in Ballybrit where the Mass was celebrated.

River Corrib: The banks of the river provide pleasant walks. As part of the new development several apartment blocks have been constructed overlooking the river.

Taibhdearc na Gaillimhe: The theatre, situated in Middle Street, is the National Theatre for plays and musicals in the Irish language.

University College, Galway: The original college, built to a similar design as Cambridge College, by Joseph B Keane was opened in 1849.

GALWAY – Spanish Arch

Salthill

Salthill is a prosperous suburb of Galway, two miles west of the city, on the shore of Galway Bay. The Irish name for Salthill is 'Bóthar na Trá', Strand Road, which is a literal description of the area. Bordered by the longest promenade in Ireland, Salthill is one of the most popular family resorts in the country. With its night clubs, amusement arcades, discos, singing pubs and a wide range of hotels and guesthouses, the area has deservedly earned itself the title 'the Blackpool of the west coast'. From the long prom, which is suitable for brisk walks winter or summer, there are superb views of Galway Bay and the Hills of Clare to the south.

According to Logan's Map of 1818, Salthill was a tiny hamlet surrounded by the seat of Mr O'Hare. At the turn of the century Salthill was cut off from Galway by fields but, with urban development buildings extended westwards to the outskirts of the city.

From the late seventeenth century medical periodicals began writing about the curative powers of salt water for those suffering from rheumatism and other ailments. As a result Salthill began to attract substantial numbers of visitors to avail of the waters. Cremin's Baths was the first of many public bath-houses built to meet the demand. In 1860 the Eglinton Hotel was the first hotel constructed in Salthill and was quickly followed by a number of medium sized hotels and guest houses. The coming of the railway to Galway brought an even greater influx of visitors.

In 1885 Alexander Moon and other Galway businessmen were responsible for erecting the first diving board at Blackrock, near the western end of the Salthill promenade. Colourful bathing boxes were set up along the beach. There were segregated swimming areas for males and females. Bishop Browne, the Catholic Bishop of Galway (1937-76) was most insistent that the sexes should be kept separate.

William Joyce, better known as 'Lord Haw-Haw' for his propaganda broadcasts from Germany during World War Two, lived for a period in Salthill. Joyce was born in Brooklyn, New York, on 24 April 1906, to Irish parents. Three years later the family returned to Ireland and in 1913 they came to live in Salthill. Educated by the Jesuits, Joyce later abandoned academic life to become a Fascist agitator. He was tried for 'high treason' and hanged in 1946. Thirty years later William Joyce was reinterred in Galway cemetery, in accordance with his dying wishes.

Donal MacAmhlaigh was born in Knocknacarra in 1926 and attended Scoil Fhursa in Salthill. In 1951 he emigrated to England to work as a navvy. He wrote an account of his work, in Irish, *Diary of an Irish Navvy*, which was later translated into English.

During the 1940s and 50s Salthill became a favourite resort, drawing hugh crowds from Ireland and Great Britain. Among the most popular sources of entertainment were the many ballrooms including The Pavilion Seapoint Ballroom and The Hangar (the latter was an aeroplane shed built at Oranmore during the First World War and later rebuilt at Salthill as a dance hall). The showband boom of the 1960s and 70s brought even larger crowds to fill the halls and dance to the music of the Royal Showband, the Dixies, the Miami, and make household names out of Brendan Bowyer, Dickie Rock and Joe Dolan.

In 1952 Salthill became a parish in its own right, having previously been part of the parish of Rahoon. The Catholic Church of Christ the King has figures of the Blessed Virgin and Sacred Heart by Oisín Kelly, a wooden Crucifixion by Claire Sheridan and three altars by Michael Scott.

Today Salthill is still a bustling resort, having lost out little to package holidays in the sun. To attract the tourists the resort has updated its facilities which include safe sandy beaches, angling, water sports, a diving board and an eighteen hole golf course. With the unpredictable Irish summers many indoor activities have been made available including a variety of amusement arcades, restaurants, musical pubs and discos. The Leisureland centre has an indoor swimming pool and stages regular musical evenings and pop concerts. Salthill Park and Quincentennial Park offer quiet havens away from the bustle. Along with its normal activities, Salthill provides two successful annual events, the Salthill Festival and the Salthill Horseshow.

RECOMMENDED:

Galway Golf Course (18 Holes).
Salthill Festival (July).
The Galleon Restaurant.
Quincenntenial Park.
La Taverna Restaurant.
Salthill Hotel.
The Hangar.
Warwick Hotel (Ballroom dancing).
Leisureland Centre.
CJs.
The Castle.
Pitch and Putt.
Squash.
Promenade.
The Rockland Hotel.
Quasar.
Hotel Sacré-Coeur.

Above: Sunset over Killary Harbour (Michael Diggin)

Left: To Inishbofin & Cromwell's castle (Jan de Fouw)

Top far left: Roundstone harbour and lobster pots (Michael Diggin)
Bottom far left: Thatched cottage (Michael Diggin)
Near left: Roundstone Harbour & Twelve Bens (Michael Diggin)

Below: Aerial view of Dún Aonghasa, Inishmore, the Aran Islands (Courtesy OPW)
Next page: Sunset over Kinvara (Tom Kelly)

The Aran Islands

The Aran Islands are a unique group of three barren islands, off the west coast of Ireland, thirty miles from Galway city. The islands, each divided by a sound are Inishmore, Inishmaan and Inisheer. They are the highest points of a limestone reef which extends from the Burren. The name Aran Islands is Oileáin Árann (The Islands of Aran) in Irish.

The landscapes of the islands are interspersed with miles of unevenly assembled stone walls. The islands have no gates and the islanders simply dislodge part of the stone wall when they are transferring livestock from one field to another. The sparse soil is mixed with seaweed for the growing of barley and potatoes.

The impression many people have of the Aran Islands is of currachs, Aran sweaters and craggy faced old men in dark clothing but much has changed in the appearance and lifestyle of the islanders. Thatched cottages are still quite common but in recent years a number of modern houses and bungalows have been erected. Kilronan, the largest village and capital of the Aran Islands, is well serviced with modern guesthouses, restaurants, pubs and craft shops. The islands are easily accessible from the mainland with ferry services from Galway, Doolin and Rossaveel and an air service with Aer Árann from Inverin.The Sea Sprinter provides an inter-island ferry service. The tourist potential has developed enormously in the past two decades with many people coming to learn or improve their Irish and others seeking a quiet relaxed holiday.

The *Annals of the Four Masters* state that the islands were initially populated 'in the 303rd year of the world,' following a great battle between the Fir Bolg and the Tuatha Dé Danann. The Fir Bolg fled to the islands following the Battle of Moytura. The stone fortresses on the islands are believed to have been built by them.

From the fifth century many monks and hermits sought out the solitude of the islands to build their churches and cells. In 483 St Énda and his companions landed on Inishmore, making it a place of prayer. He founded a monastery and was joined there by the founders of other churches and monasteries including Brendan the Navigator, Jarlath of Tuam, Ciarán of Clonmacnoise, Finnian of Moville, Colman and Colmcille. The islands gained the title 'Aran of the Saints.' There are reputed to be 120 graves of saints at Killeany (Cill Éinne).

In 1019 the Vikings invaded the islands and captured 150 islanders. Two years later there was large scale death from a colic plague. In 1020 there were further attacks by the Vikings in which the monastic settlement was plundered and burned.

By the late 1200s the islands were under the control of the O'Briens, the Munster sept, who were descendants of Brian Boru. The O'Briens were fierce warriors, acting as protectors of Galway Bay. They showed no mercy to pirates, killing the crews and capturing their weapons and valuables. They were paid an annual levy of twelve tuns of wine for their services. The O'Briens built a castle within a large ringfort on Inisheer, and a Franciscan house at Killeany.

In 1400 the O'Briens joined forces with the Galway pirates against the forces of King Henry IV. The alliance did not last but the O'Briens continued to dominate Aran for almost the next two centuries. In 1585 feuding among the O'Briens resulted in the O'Flahertys of Iar Connacht driving them from the islands. In 1587 Queen Elizabeth expelled the O'Flahertys and granted the islands to Sir John Rawson on condition that he garrisoned the islands and built a castle on Inishmore which would protect the entrance to Galway port. He subsequently built Arkin Castle beside the shore in 1587.

legendary pirate queen

In the 1540s Grace O'Malley, the pirate queen, raided the islands with a fleet of boats. Her son-in-law, the Devil's Hook, insisted she return the spoils and so she narrowly escaped hanging. In 1614 during a visit, Oliver St John, a courtier, reported that English and Portuguese vessels fished the waters around the islands.

In 1641 the O'Briens joined with Boetius Clancy the Younger, a wealthy businessman from County Clare, and with a large force prepared an attack on the islands but the Marquis of Clanrickard, Governor of County Galway, intervened and prevented the rising. That same year Murrough O'Flaherty and a large force travelled to Inisheer where they rested before attacking Tromoe Castle in Clare. John Browne of Inisheer, one of the raiding party, is said to have informed on Murrough, who was hanged twelve years later by Cromwellian forces.

In 1651 two hundred troops under Sir Robert Lynch, were stationed on the islands to defend them from Parliamentary forces. Cannons were placed on Arkynes Fort. In 1652 Galway surrendered to the Parliamentary forces but it was a year later, on 15 January, that Aran finally capitulated to Cromwellian forces. The troops demolished Arkin Castle and replaced it with a fortress, using stones from the suppressed monastery. Many of the priests were transported to the West Indies. They were granted an allowance of six pence per day as they awaited transportation. In 1662 the islands were granted to Richard Butler, who was appointed First Earl of Aran. The following year Captain Bayly was appointed governor of 'The Isles of Arran and Boffin.'

In 1687 the Catholic James II granted 75% of the tithes of the Aran Islands to the Church of Ireland Archbishop Vesey of Tuam and to his successors. In 1691 a barracks was built on Inishmore. In 1708 Richard Wall, Mayor of Galway, despatched a strong force of troops to defend Aran against a possible French invasion. The invasion never materialised but the force was maintained to protect the islands against French pirates.

From about 1740 the Digby family of Kildare became the islands' landlords but were in the main absent and only took rent. Many islanders were unable to pay their rent and were evicted. In 1745 a dispute arose when John Digby harpooned a whale off Aran and the Mayor of Galway claimed the mammal and its oil, but Digby persevered and kept his bounty.

The 1800s were to be a depressing period for Aran with successive failures of the potato crop and large scale emigration with the population decreasing from 3521 in 1841 to 1496 in 1976. There was a determination by the islanders, despite official pressure, to maintain Irish as the first language of the people. Conditions became so critical that in 1886 Fr O'Donoghue, a local priest, made a plea to the authorities to 'send us boats or send us coffins.' The request was heeded and five years later the Congested Districts Board (set up by the Government to help establish small industries and relieve poverty) began to stimulate the fishing industry. They built piers and a steamer service was inaugurated from Galway to Kilronan, which became a fishing port.

Liam O'Flaherty (1896 - 1984)

Máirtín Ó Direáin (1910 -)

In the early nineteenth century Patrick O'Flaherty was 'the uncrowned King of Aran'. He served as a judge for wrongdoers, sentencing some to Galway Jail. During the friction of the Land War some of O'Flaherty's cattle were deliberately driven over a cliff.

At the turn of the century, with the Irish literary revival, Aran had visits from many literary figures seeking inspiration. The Yeats brothers, W B and Jack, brought pen and brush respectively, Lady Gregory spent several periods on the islands and, above all, John Millington Synge discovered there ingredients for several plays and produced a fine book, *The Aran Islands* in 1905. The islands were to produce their own distinguished writers. Liam O'Flaherty was born in the small village of Gortnagapple on Inishmore in 1897. He was brought up in an Irish-speaking family and served in the British Army during World War One. He was to become a leading writer of short stories and novels in Irish and English. His best known works are *The Informer, Skerrett, Insurrection* and *The Black Soul*. He died in 1984. Máirtín Ó Direáin was born on Aran in 1910. During World War Two he was employed in Postal Censorship. He was to become one of 'the most powerful Irish poets' of his time and produced such collections as Rogha Dánta and Cloch Choirnéil. Brendán Ó hEithir, born on Aran in 1930 was to gain distinction as a journalist, broadcaster and author. Among his works are *Over the Bar* and *Thar Ghealchathair Soir.*

On a boat trip from America to Europe, the renowned documentary film maker, Robert Flaherty, heard a young Irishman tell of the Aran Islands, where life was so primitive that the islanders had to make soil

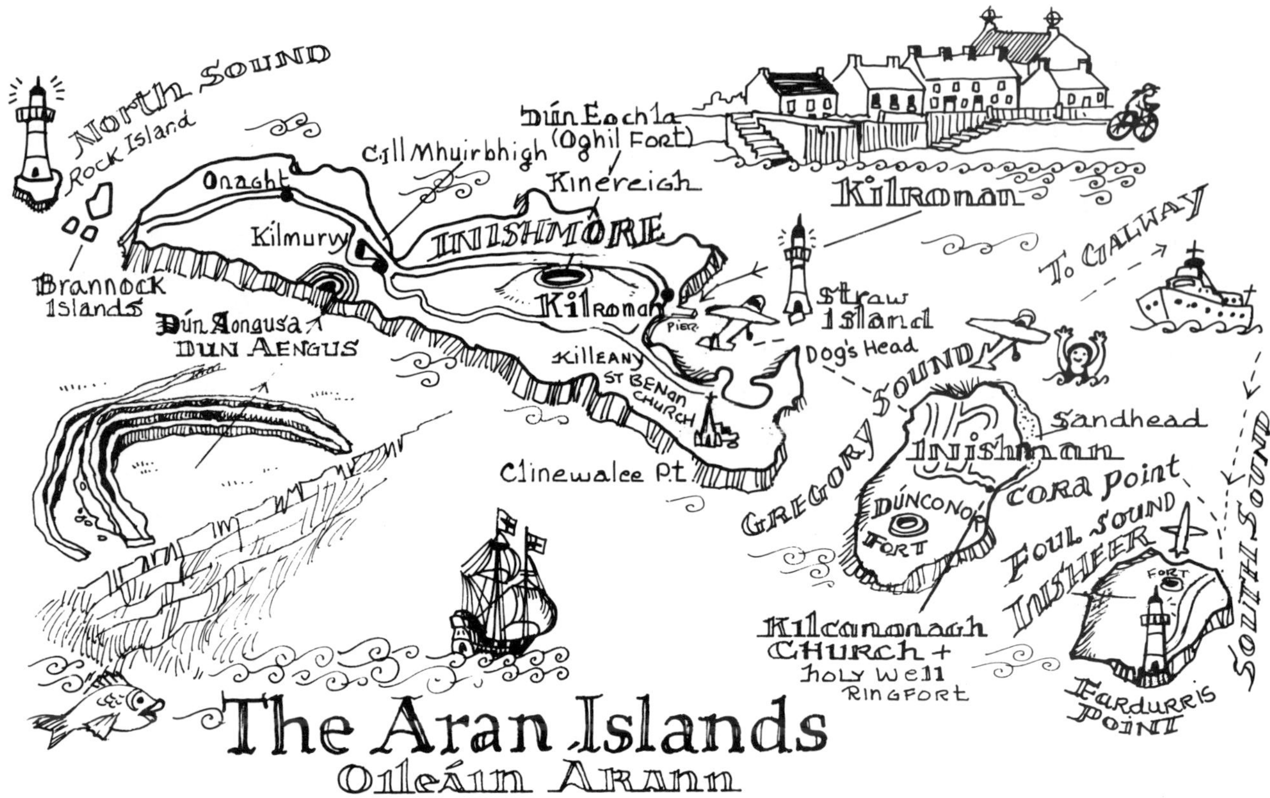

by hauling seaweed up the cliffs and mixing it with sand to form a top-soil. This impressed Flaherty and he saw it as man's struggle against the elements and began to research the subject. Michael Balcon, production chief of Gaumont-British, allotted £10,000 for *Man of Aran*, as a sound film, which was less than the cost of Flaherty's silent film Nanook of the North, made a decade before. Flaherty cast islanders in all the roles, Mikaleen Dillane, as the boy; Maggie Dirrane as the mother; and the most difficult character to cast, the father, was finally found in the person of Tiger King. Flaherty commenced filming in 1932. The islanders, for people who astonishingly could not swim, performed the most incredible feats of bravery, encouraged by Flaherty's unsparing energy. In the film, he gambled with the lives of people living at starvation level and was in constant fear that tragedy would strike. The film won the Grand Prix Award at the Venice Film Festival — and a secure place in the history of cinema as one of the greatest documentaries of all time.

In the past Aran has been noted for its distinctive clothing. Some of the men still wear a waistcoat of unbleached wool, called a báinín. Many men wear dark, thick tweed trousers. Aran sweaters have long been associated with the islanders. The women used to knit the sweaters in family patterns in order to identify drowned fishermen. There is still a lucrative market for white sweaters with intricate designs in America and on the continent. Other items of traditional apparel are the Aran crios, a belt of coloured woven wools, worn around the waist and pampooties, moccasin-type soft shoes. The thick woollen shawl and red flannel skirt, as worn in John Millington Synge's *The Playboy of the Western World*, are now only worn on festive occasions.

The currach is still the most utilised craft on the islands. It is a light craft made of laths and canvas and sealed with tar, which the fishermen handle with precision. Synge wrote of the currach: 'It is a moment of exquisite satisfaction to find myself moving away from civilisation in this crude canvas canoe of a model that has served primitive races since men first went to sea.'

Inishmore

Inishmore, eight miles long and two miles wide, is the largest of the Aran Islands, with a population of about 900. The name Inishmore in Irish is Inis Mór (Big Island).

The island is noted for its large stone forts. The climb up the path west of the village of Kilmurvey (Cill Mhuirbhigh), to the fort of Dún Aengus (Dún Aonghasa), with its sheer drop to the Atlantic, is for many the highlight of their visit to Aran. A mile and a half west of Killeany (Cill Éinne), on the southern side, is Dubh-Chathair, another stone fort and Dún Eochla (Oghil Fort), a circular structure, is the highest point on the island, standing 300 feet above sea level. There are also christian chapels, shrines, standing stones and clocháns scattered around the island.

Other important sites on the island include St Benan's church, an ancient oratory, one of the smallest in Ireland. At the location known as The Seven Churches, there are only the remains of two churches, dating back to the eighth century. St Fursey, St Conal, St Brecan and St Brendan were associated with Teampall an Cheathrair Álainn (The Church of the Four Beautiful Saints).

Kilronan, the capital and port of the islands, is a small village situated at the eastern end of Inishmore. The village takes its name, Cill Rónáin (the Church of Ronan), from St Ronan, of whom the only relic is Leaba Rónáin, the Saints bed or grave. Halla Rónáin, the parish hall, serves as a theatre, community hall and cinema. During the summer months there are several screenings daily of the film, *Man of Aran.* Kilronan, the island's administrative centre, is connected by road to a number of smaller villages. The stone pier affords shelter to the modern fishing boats and a docking place for ferries from Galway and Rossaveel. From Kilronan the visitor can tour the island. The most reliable means of transport are bicycles which can be hired on the island at Aran Bike Hire and Kilronan Bicycle Hire, both in Kilronan. Mini-coach tours are available from Máirtin Mullin. There are a number of small beaches on the island.

On 15 August 1852, fifteen fishermen were drowned, fourteen from Killeany. They had been fishing under the cliffs when a freak wave swept them out to sea. From the mid-nineteenth century the small Protestant community lived close to Kilronan where the Episcopalian Church of St Thomas was erected. In 1891 a steamer service was inaugurated from Galway to Kilronan.

Ionad Árann, Aran's Heritage Centre, is located at Kilronan. The centre introduces the visitor to the culture, traditions and landscapes of the islands and is open from Easter to September.

RECOMMENDED

Tourist Office.
Aran's Heritage Centre.
Inis Mór Campsite.
Halla Ronáin.
Aran Bike Hire.
Dún Aonghasa.
Dún Eochla.
Dubh-Chathair
Daily screening of 'Man of Aran'.
Kilmurvey House.
Bayview House B&B and Restaurant.
Mullen's Cottage Craft.
Kilronan Bicycle Hire.
Mainistir House Hostel.
The Man of Aran Cottage Tearooms.
Joe Mac's Pub.
Dún Aengus Restaurant, Kilronan.
An tSean-Cheibh Restaurant.

Inishmaan

Inishmaan is the middle island and the most barren and remote, with a rocky shore and high cliffs. The Irish name for Inishmaan is Inis Meáin (The Middle Island). The island is separated from Inishmore by Gregory's Sound and is the least visited of the islands and one which most retains the traditional lifestyle. Seven little villages form a continuous band of settlement across the island.

Inishmaan only has a population of approximately 300 people, one pub, a community hall and a post office. The island has an airstrip where Aer Árann runs regular trips to and from Inverin. Boats from the other islands and the mainland dock at An Cora Pier. Near the pier is Trá Leitreach, a safe beach for swimming.

The huge fort of Dún Conor, Dún Conchúir (Conor's Fort), is visible from the sound as the boat approaches the island. After Dún Aonghasa, this is the largest and most impressive of all the Aran forts and perhaps dates to the first century AD. From the fort there is a panoramic view of the island. Another good viewing point is a hill in the centre of the island. Near the boat landing area are the ruins of Kilcanonagh Church, a small simple building. Closeby there is a holy well and a stone ringfort. Northeast of the village of An Mothair (Mohair), there is a chamber tomb known as Leaba Dhiarmada (Dermot and Gráinne's Bed). South of this site is Saint Cinndheirg's Well which is reputed to have curative powers. Teampall na Seacht Mac Rí is another ancient church but sadly only the foundations remain.

As with Inishmore the atmosphere of the island can be best savoured on foot. Recommended walks are: to the western shore; east to Cora Point and to Sandhead in the northeast. There is a pony and trap which will take visitors on a tour of the island. Make sure you agree the fare in advance of the trip. At the end of An Mothair is the Catholic church in which James Pearse, father of Pádraig, designed the altar. The windows by Harry Clarke are worth viewing.

The playwright, John Millington Synge, spent each summer from 1898 to 1902 on Inishmaan and studied the life pattern of the people. The cottage where Synge stayed is today signposted as Teach Synge. He set his great drama of the sea, *Riders to the Sea*, on Inishmaan. On the cliffs near Dún Beag there is a stony location named Cathaoir Synge (Synge's Chair) where the playwright would meditate. The Synge Weekend held each July is an enjoyable mixture of lectures, drama and music.

One feature of Inishmaan, of which the islanders are extremely proud, is the knitwear factory. This co-operative exports high class knitwear worldwide. The Folk Museum is worth a visit to learn something of the history of the life, dress and customs of the islanders.

RECOMMENDED

Folk Museum.
Kilcanonagh Church.
Dún Conor.
Synge Weekend (July).
An Dún Restaurant.
Teach Synge.
Leaba Dhiarmada.
Cathaoir Synge.

Inisheer

Inisheer is the smallest and most easterly of the Aran Islands, divided from Inishmaan by Foul Sound. The island is only about two miles long and about 1 $^{1}/_{2}$ miles wide and has two main roads, one running from south to north and the second extending from East Village to the pier. The name Inisheer in Irish is Inis Oírr (Eastern Island).

Boats from the other islands or the mainland dock at the landing slip on the northern shore. There is a castle and a number of interesting churches on the island. In the late fourteenth century the tower castle was erected in a stone fort which dates back to a thousand years earlier. West of the docking area there is a tenth century church, known as Kilgobnet, dedicated to St Gobnait, the only woman allowed on the island among the holy men. Close by there is Knockgrannia, a Bronze Age burial place. Two miles south of the castle there is an ancient graveyard, known as Cill na Seacht nIníon (the church of the Seven Daughters). To the southeast are the ruins of St Cavan's church, an early structure. St Cavan's Grave is reputed to be nearby in the sand.

In the summer of 1931 Orson Welles, the great American actor/director, then sixteen years old, stayed on Inisheer for some weeks, while he toured the west coast on a horse and cart. Later that year, he travelled to Dublin, where he convinced Micheál Mac Liammóir and Hilton Edwards that he was an established American actor and they cast him in a number of plays in the Gate Theatre.

A folk museum has been built on the island which consists of a thatched cottage, a craft shop, a gallery with old photographs, books and tearooms. Once again walking is the best method of seeing the island. One interesting walk is from the East Village down to the lighthouse at Fardurris Point. The Aer Árann airfield is situated on the northern side of the island. Tigh Ned and Tigh Ruairí are two good atmospheric pubs and the Fisherman's Cottage Restaurant is to be recommended, especially for fresh seafood.

RECOMMENDED

Óstan Inis Oírr.
Tigh Ruairi Pub.
O'Brien's Castle.
Camping Site.
Aer Árann airstrip.
Fisherman's Cottage Restaurant.
The Heritage House.
Tigh Ned.
Dúchas Inis Oírr, Cultural Holiday Courses.
Radharc na Mara Hostel.

Right: the distinctive currach (traditional rowing boat)

South Connemara

On paper, Connemara, with its extensive bogs, mountains and many narrow, potholed roads, would appear to be the most unlikely destination for tourists. In reality the opposite is true and Connemara is one of the most interesting and most frequently visited areas in the entire country.

Connemara is the western portion of County Galway and extends from Killary Harbour in the north, across the Maamturk Mountains to the east, southwards to Kilkieran Bay and along the jagged Atlantic inlets. Connemara, which is dominated by the two mountain ranges of the Twelve Bens and the Maamturks and many meandering rivers and streams, is one of the most unspoilt areas in Ireland. There are vast tracts of bog, and turf is harvested in spring and summer to fuel the homes of the locals. Traces of the early history of the area are evident in the many standing stones, ringforts, crannógs and megalithic tombs scattered across the landscape. The stark tapestry of bog, lakes, valleys and mountains combines with the beauty spots of Kylemore, Lough Inagh and Claddaghduff to make the images of Connemara remain long in the memory.

The Connemara pony which usually stands at 14.2 hands high is unique to this area and is particularly suited as a children's pony. They can be viewed to best advantage at the Connemara Pony Show. Another animal very much associated with the area is the sheep and many unmistakeable profiles dot the countryside from seashore to mountain face.

This segment of the book covers most of the towns and villages of South Connemara and a portion of West Galway. Commencing at Barna, the traveller proceeds westwards along the coast road through the Gaeltacht areas. Spiddal is the most popular stopping place for a good pint, a meal or to sample Irish culture in the form of music, dancing, drama and, of course, the Irish language. The road continues through the wild, sparsely populated countryside to Carraroe with its coral beach and the unspoilt islands of Lettermore, Gorumna and Lettermullen and on to Carna. From Carna the road extends northwards to connect with the main Clifden to Galway Road at Recess. The traveller can then continue in a horse-shoe direction through the major angling and golfing village of Oughterard, skirting Lough Corrib to Moycullen, noted for its Connemara marble and high class restaurants. The roads are, in the main, level and suitable for cyclists and cars but coaches would be advised to avoid some of the more westerly boreens.

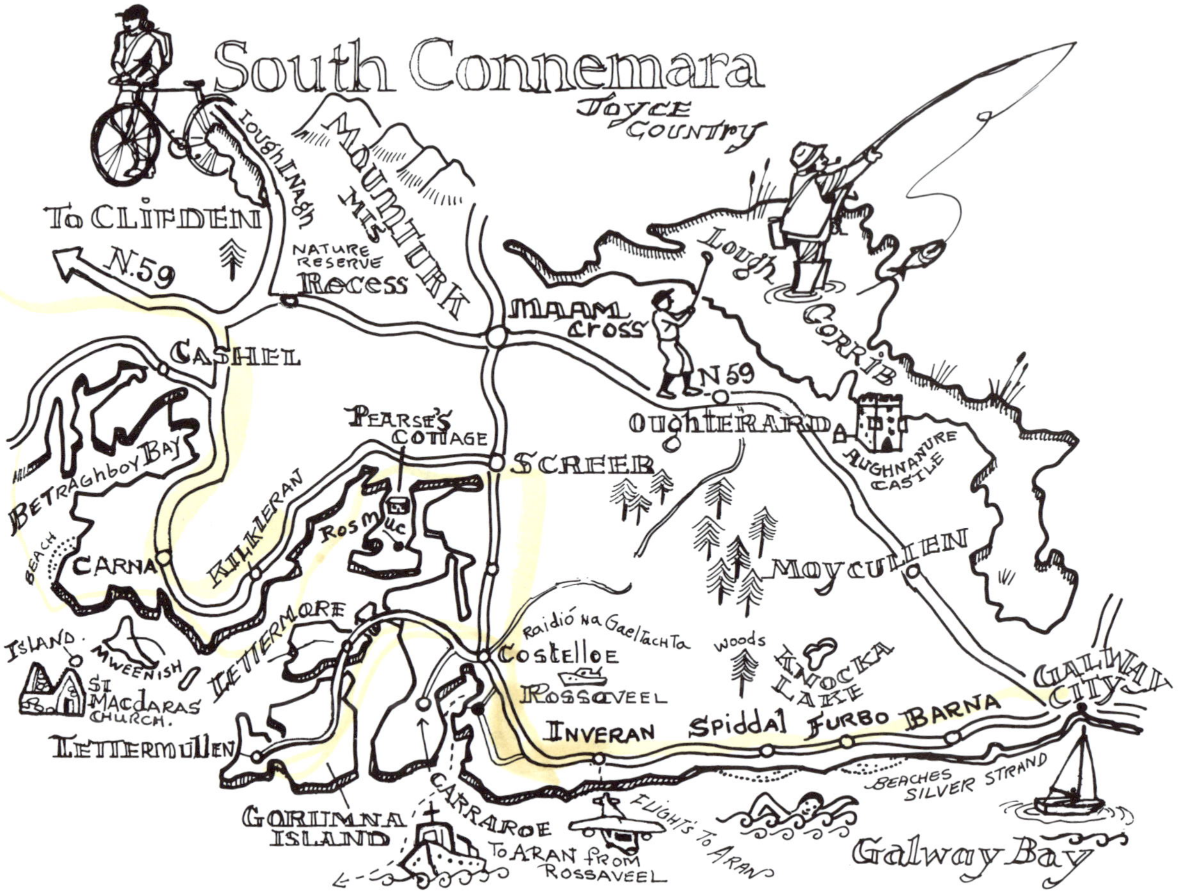
South Connemara
Joyce Country
Lough Inagh
Maumturk Mts
To CLIFDEN
N.59
Nature Reserve
Recess
Maam Cross
Lough Corrib
N59
Oughterard
Aughnanure Castle
Cashel
Pearse's Cottage
Screeb
Betraghboy Bay
Kilkieran
Rosmuc
Beach
Carna
Moycullen
Raidió na Gaeltachta
Costelloe
Woods
Knocka Lake
Island
Mweenish
St Macdaras Church
Lettermore
Rossaveel
Galway City
Lettermullen
Inveran
Spiddal
Furbo
Barna
Beaches
Silver Strand
Gorumna Island
Carraroe
Flights to Aran
To Aran from Rossaveel
Galway Bay

G.210

Barna

Barna is a small village on the coast road, five miles west of Galway city, on the main Galway to Carraroe Road. The name Barna in Irish is Bearna (a Gap or Mountain Gap). On entering the village from the Galway side, Barna Woods lie to the right and the left hand turn takes the traveller to the sheltered sandy beach at Silver Strand. On the western side of the village there are further safe beaches. For those interested in fishing or sailing, the pier head offers facilities for mooring boats and yachts. There is a crossroads in the centre of the village, on two corners of which are Donnelly's Bar and the Twelve Pins Bar and Restaurant. Both premises were built around 1800. The Pier Road has several interesting venues including An Gailearai Beag, Ty Ar Mór Restaurant and 'Stone Sculpture'. Barna is the beginning of the Gaeltacht area which extends westwards to Carna.

Around the twelfth century the O'Halloran family, who were Lords of Clan Fergail, built a castle close to the sea, which was known as the Old Castle of Barna. In 1588, following the wrecking of several ships of the Spanish Armada off the west coast, seventy surviving Spaniards put ashore at Barna to seek assistance. They were taken prisoner by the British, under Richard Bingham and brought to Galway, where they were executed. A century later the road from the Claddagh was extended over Feeney's Marsh to Barna. The marsh later became a bird sanctuary.

In the 1770s Marcus Blake Lynch built the imposing Barna House, overlooking the Silver Strand. Shortly afterwards the Lynch family initiated the building of a number of thatched cottages and the village proper began to develop. According to the 1812 Census there was a population of 560 in Barna. This comprised fifty-four families, twenty-two of whom were engaged in agriculture and the remainder in fishing and other labouring work. In the 1820s Alexander Nimmo, the Scottish civil engineer, who spent £167,000 on roads and piers in Connemara, built Barna Pier. Around 1830, the Roman Catholic Church of St James, was built and paid for by the Lynch family, the local Catholic landlords. This building replaced the old thatched roof school. The Lynchs also built the boys' school. Around this period a soup kitchen for the needy was opened on the pier.

On Sunday 14 November 1920, Fr Michael Griffin, a young curate in Barna, responded to a bogus sick call. Six days later, his body was found in a shallow grave, outside the village. He had been shot in the head. There was outrage in the community at the murder. Locals were firmly convinced that the Black and Tans were responsible for his death but it

Facing page (bottom): Rossaveel harbour

could never be proved. North of Barna, on the Moycullen Road, there is a memorial honouring Fr Griffin. In 1922 during the Civil War two pubs and the coastguard station in the village were destroyed by arson.

Several well known people have had connections with Barna. In 1920 the writer, Éilís Dillon, who was born in Galway, moved with her family to live at Barna Pier. Her father was professor of chemistry at University College, Galway. Her mother was the former Geraldine Plunkett. Eilís Dillon married Cormac Ó Cuilleánain, professor of Irish at University College, Cork; their daughter, Eileán Ní Chuilleánain is a well-known poet. After her husband's death in 1970 Eilís married Vivian Mercier, the critic and professor of English at the University of California. Eilís went on to become a prolific writer of novels and children's books. Joseph Pilkington, the actor, best known for his part as Eamon Maher, in the popular RTE television series, *The Riordans,* was born in Eagle Lodge, Barna.

Until 1952 Barna/Furbo was part of the parish of Rahoon. Barna then became part of the new Salthill parish. In 1972 Barna became a parish in its own right. Five years later a new church was erected in Barna.

Close to the village is St Enda's Well which was once a place of pilgrimage. The well is believed to be where St Enda stopped on the way to the Aran Islands. The village has several good class restaurants including The Twelve Pins Restaurant, Donnelly's Restaurant and Ty Ar Mór Restaurant.

Eílís Dillon (1920 – 1994)

RECOMMENDED

Barna Caravan Park.
Barna Youth Club.
Barna Woods.
Timber Leaves (Wood craft).
The Twelve Pins Restaurant.
Mary Immaculate Queen Catholic Church.
Galway Bay Cottages.
Ty Ar Mór Restaurant.
An Gailearai Beag.
Donnelly's Bar and Restaurant.
Silver Strand.

Furbo

From Barna the road continues westwards to the small coastal village of Furbo. The name Furbo in Irish is Na Forbacha (Rough Lands). Along this stretch there is a rugged coast line running parallel with the main road. Close to the village is a safe, sandy beach, overlooked by a car park.

The name Furbo is first mentioned in the reign of Queen Elizabeth I when she granted 500 acres of land to Marcus Lynch Gibbon. In 1699 a travel writer gave a description of the area: 'Six miles beyond Galway is a place called "Lynch's Folly", from the extravagant design of the owner who endeavoured to raise a mount in his garden to such a height as to overtop a high mountain at the foot of which it is situated, in order to have a view of the sea and the neighbouring.'

In 1841 the Blake family built Furbo House from limestone, which was transported by boat from County Clare. The family, who owned much of the surrounding townlands, also built Furbo Pier and a lime burning kiln which was used for agricultural purposes. That same year, Edmond Blake, a Blake of Furbo, became Mayor of Galway. Galway Corporation were unable to pay his arrears of salary and instead allowed him to retain the sword and mace. Following his death, his property passed to his daughter, Anne Blake of Murrough House, Furbo. Furbo House is in ruins today. Later, Andrew Blake, who was High Sheriff of Galway, built Marino House in Furbo.

Another member of the family, Seán Buí Blake or 'Seán Sunday', as he was commonly known, lived in a smaller house nearby. He acted as a bailiff for his brother and only appeared on Sunday; nobody could be issued with a warrant that day. One Sunday in 1882 he was shot dead coming from Mass. The Blakes, who ran a pack of beagles, were not popular landlords. During a famine in the 1870s Fr Peter Daly, a local curate, set up a soup kitchen at the gate of Marino House, to alleviate the plight of the hungry. The Blakes were far from pleased with his action. There was a change of attitude in later years and the Blakes built a family mausoleum in Furbo and provided land and finance for the chapel in 1933.

Furbo is the National headquarters of Udaras na Gaeltachta, the Gaeltacht Development Authority. Situated next to their building are the offices of Rionn na Gaeltachta, the State department responsible for the Gaeltacht affairs, decentralised from Dublin in the early 1980s.

In 1951 Bord Fáilte sold Marino House to George McCambridge. In 1968 the building changed hands again and was bought by Bill Fuller, who opened it as Teach Furbo, a popular hotel for music. In recent years the hotel has been extensively modernised and enlarged and it is now known as Connemara Coast Hotel. Tigh Phadraicín is a favourite music pub in the district.

RECOMMENDED

Knocka Lough (fishing).
Connemara Coast Hotel.
Marino Holiday Cottages.
Furbo Woods.
Beach.
Tigh Phadraicín.
Pony Trekking.

Below: Spiddal street scenes (Arthur Flynn)

Spiddal

Farther west and ten miles from Galway city is the lively village of Spiddal. The name Spiddal in Irish is An Spidéal, derived from Ospidéal (Hospital). The Knights Hospitalers are believed to have established a hospital here around the fourteenth century. Close to the village there is a bridge over the Boluisce River. In early times the village was also known as Baile an Droichid (the Town of the Bridge). The beach is located beside the Catholic church. There is excellent fishing and swimming in the area and the large sheltered pier head has good mooring facilities. Some traditional white- washed cottages still exist near the village.

For those seeking out traditional music sessions and set dancing Cruiscin Lán and Tigh Hughes are a must. Spiddal is on the edge of the Connemara Gaeltacht and many shops and business premises trade under their Irish names. Irish is spoken freely among the locals in their homes, workplaces and schools.

About a mile east of the village is Coláiste Chonnacht, founded in 1909, one of the oldest Irish colleges in the country which attracts hundreds of students each summer to study the language. The students stay in the homes of local families. An Gael-Acadamh organises musical and cultural events during the year. Another feature of the area is the currach, a small traditional craft which is still used by local men for fishing and transporting goods. Every June Féile na gCurrach (Festival of the Currachs) offers an exciting spectacle.

East of the village, in the late seventeenth century, Roderick O'Flaherty built a large house called Park. He was to distinguish himself as an antiquary, and wrote *Ogygia, a Latin History of Ireland.* In 1718 he died in poverty and was buried beside the house. In 1776 Stephen Martin erected a small Protestant church in the area. It has not been used for many years.

On the right hand side of the main road is Spiddal House, situated in a magnificent wooded demesne. The property was once known as Bothua and was part of the Blake estate. The house was built at the beginning of the nineteenth century for the Morris family, who were landlords of the village. During the Civil War of 1922 the house was burned but was rebuilt five years later. One of the best known members of the Morris family is Lord Killanin, son of Martin Morris. Lord Killanin became a film producer and is a former President of the International Olympic Committee.

In 1904 Cill Einde, St Énda's Catholic Church, was built to a design by William A. Scott. The building is Celtic Romanesque in style, a revival of an important period of Irish architecture. Sarah Purser designed four of the church's windows. In the adjoining cemetery are the remains of the old parish church. Closer to the sea there is a small thirteenth century church, still in good repair. Just outside the village is The Mass Rock, Carraig an Aifreann, which was used during Penal Days.

The film director, John Ford (registered at birth as Sean O'Fearna, and later as O'Feeney) was born in America on 1 February 1895, the thirteenth child of Irish immigrants from Spiddal. He was to gain fame as one of the world's most distinguished film directors, directing such classic films as *Stagecoach* and *The Informer*. In 1951 John Ford spent many pleasant periods in Spiddal with John Wayne, visiting relatives, while filming *The Quiet Man*, in Cong. In the early 1980s, scenes for a major American television series, *The Mannions of America*, starring Pierce Brosnan and David Soul, were filmed in the Spiddal area. In 1992, the twelve part 'Ros na Rón', had the distinction of being the first television soap opera completely in Irish. It was partly filmed around Spiddal. There are a number of television and video production companies operating in the Gaeltacht. One of these, Telegael, is situated in the old parochial house in Spiddal.

In the townland of An Cnocán Glas, west of the village, is the birthplace of Máirtín Ó Cadhain, a noted prose writer in Irish. He was born in the village in 1907 and became a teacher and a member of the IRA in the 1930s. During the Second World War he spent five years in the Curragh Internment Camp. His books include *Idir Shugradh agus Dáirire, An Braon Broghach* and *Cré na Cille*. He died in 1970.

A place not to be missed is Ceardlann an Spidéil, (Spiddal Craft Centre), where craftworkers can be observed in action. Their produce can be purchased. Among the crafts on display are woodturning, screenprinting, weaving, stonework, knitwear and pottery. Along with the Irish language, pubs and traditional music, there is also a centre for Aquasport, an Angling School and Spiddal Animal Farm, which is much enjoyed by children. For those without transport it is worth checking out the list of trips on offer from Ó Neachtain Coach Tours.

RECOMMENDED

Village Hostel.
Ceardlann an Spidéil
Angling School.
Park Lodge Hotel.
Aquasport An Spideal.
Cruiscin Lan.
Currach Festival (June).
Pairc Saoire an Spidéil (Caravan Park).
Spiddal Holiday Homes.
Tigh Hughes (Traditional Music).
Ceol na Mara.
Public Library.
Beach.
Spiddal Animal Farm.
Coláiste Chonnacht.
Standún.
Craft Shop.
Ó Neachtain Coach Tours

Inverin

The small coastal village of Inverin is about four miles west of Spiddal on the main Galway to Carraroe Road. The name in Irish is Indreabhán (River Mouth). Several minor roads lead to the seashore where there is a good sandy beach which is suitable for swimming and fishing.

Close to the village there is an old cemetery where once stood a church dedicated to St Colmcille. According to tradition when St Colmcille sailed from Aran he landed at Inverin.

New bungalows are interspersed with traditional cottages. There has been a renewed interest in thatched cottages and some are being rebuilt and rethatched. Feelings for the Irish language are so strongly held by some in the community that the English names on many road signs have been painted out. Coláiste Lurgan, an Irish college, is situated in the locality. It offers summer courses for students. The Bay Language School holds intensive courses in English and German. All locals, whether on foot, bike, car or tractor wave and salute and make strangers feel welcome.

In 1917, during the First World War, a German war mine was washed up on the beach at Inverin. When a group of local men went to investigate the mine exploded, killing nine of them. A monument has been erected at the site in their memory. Further along the seashore there is a children's burial ground, in which the last burials took place early this century. Close to the burial ground is a holy well. Micheál Breathnach, a writer and Gaelic scholar was born in the vicinity in 1881 and a memorial marks his birthplace.

Aer Árann Connemara Airport is situated at Inverin and runs daily flights to all three Aran Islands. The airline was established in 1970 and flights to the islands only take six minutes. Pleasure flights can also be booked from the airport. An Óige Hostel is situated at the turn to Aer Árann Airport. There are holiday homes for renting in the area. The Poitín Stil Pub is a popular venue for night time entertainment. Turn at the Poitín Stil for a signposted bogland walk by Loch Cheara, with its plentiful wildlife. The Joyce Country Way Drive also begins at Inverin. The studios for Teilifís na Gaeilge will be centred in the area.

Roger Corman, the American film-maker, is to establish a film studio close by to produce films for the international market.

RECOMMENDED

Explosion Memorial.
Beach.
Aer Árann Airport.
An Óige Hostel.
Poitín Stil Pub.
Loch Cheara.
The Joyce Way Drive.
Children's Burial Place.

Rossaveel

From Inverin a minor road left takes the traveller to Rossaveel, a small village with a rapidly developing harbour. Funded by a European Community grant, the new harbour incorporates the Rossaveel Fishery Harbour Centre and the new quays. A cold store, an auction room and a fish processing factory have been added in recent years, making it the most important fishing harbour of County Galway. The name Rossaveel in Irish is Ros An Mhíl (The Peninsula of the Whale or Sea-Monster).

There is an ongoing trade and boat service from Rossaveel to the Aran Islands. For many years 'The Queen of Aran' cabin cruiser ran regular passenger services to the islands. Today the service is provided by the 'Aran Flyer' ferry with a twenty minute crossing. Passengers may travel by bus from Galway and car owners can leave their vehicles in the large car park beside the harbour.

For many centuries there was no fuel on the Aran Islands and hookers, the traditional wooden sail boats of Connemara, took supplies of turf from Rossaveel. The attractive Catholic Church, Cill Treasa Naofa an Linbh, situated on a hilltop, was constructed in 1933.

There are still old thatched cottages in the vicinity, in varying states of repair. Tigh Terry can be recommended for a good night of traditional music or country and western. And nearby is the thatched pub Tigh Johnny Sheáin. For such a small community there are two good restaurants in the village, Le Morganou and An Gleiteog. A note of warning to drivers. Travel carefully as the roads are littered with potholes and a single miscalculation on a bend could leave your car nose first in a bog.

RECOMMENDED

Le Morganou Restaurant.
Catholic Church.
Harbour.
Aran Flyer Ferry.
An Gleoiteog Restaurant.
Tigh Terry.
Tigh Johnny Sheáin.

Costelloe

Taking a north-eastern course, return to the main Galway to Carraroe road. At the small village of Costelloe the road leads northwards to Screeb and Maam Cross and the left hand turn brings the traveller to Carraroe. The name Costelloe in Irish is Casla (Sea Inlet). Locally, the village is more often referred to by its Irish title.

The barren landscape of rock and bog between Inverin and Costelloe is only broken by an unsightly series of telegraph poles and an occasional grazing sheep. The Casla River, which flows from Lough Glenicmurrin into Casla Bay, is a favourite location for trout and salmon fishermen. There are also many prime fishing lakes in the district including Lough Formoyle, Lough Glenicmurrin and Lough Cloonadoon. In 1804 a Martello tower was erected at the edge of Casla Bay as a watch tower against a possible French invasion.

Costelloe is where J Bruce Ismay, Chairman and Managing Director of the White Star Line which owned the ill-fated Titanic, fled to avoid the press in April 1912 after the sinking of the liner, with the loss of 1500 lives. Ismay was a passenger on board the Titanic during her maiden voyage from Southampton to New York. There was controversy as to why Ismay had boarded a lifeboat with so many passengers still on board. He bought Costelloe Lodge and experienced recurring nightmares of the tragedy. The building is now Costelloe Lodge Fishing Club.

Costelloe is the national headquarters for Raidió na Gaeltachta, the state-sponsored Irish-speaking radio service, which was established in 1972. The station has local transmitters in studios in County Kerry and County Donegal and is broadcast nationwide on VHF/FM and on Medium wave 556M in Connemara.

RECOMMENDED

O'Flaherty's Pub.
Dunlann Gallery.
Casla River.
Raidió na Gaeltachta.
Costelloe Lodge Fishing Club.
Lough Formoyle.
Lough Glenicmurrin.

Carraroe

From Costelloe the traveller should take a left hand turn and follow the road due south to Carraroe, which is another small coastal village, thirty miles west of Galway city. There is a rich culture of language, music and dance in the village which is a Gaeltacht area where Irish is spoken. The name in Irish is An Cheathrú Rua (The Red-Coloured Quarter).

Carraroe is situated on a peninsula and offers an abundance of safe beaches including the Coral Strand or Trá an Dóilín. The village is one of the country's most popular Irish-speaking centres for family holidays. There are three Irish colleges in the village where students can learn or improve their Irish. Students stay in the homes of villagers and only speak Irish during their stay.

In 1880 the people of Carraroe fought to have a branch line of the Galway to Clifden railway line extended to Carraroe but the Midland Great Western Railway Company were unwilling to provide the service. During the Land War, in June 1881 members of the Royal Irish Constabulary and bailiffs evicted two families on property belonging to J S Kirwan at Carraroe, for non-payment of rent. British gunboats arrived off the coast to assist with the evictions.

A strong tradition in this part of Connemara, for many centuries, has been the boats use of as trading vessels to transport passengers, turf and cargo to Kinvara and the Aran Islands. These wooden sailing vessels with large tarred hulls and red-brown sails are called hookers. Each August Cruinniú na mBád (Gathering of the Boats) is celebrated when a fleet of Hookers, gaff-rigged workboats, loaded with turf, race across Galway Bay to Kinvara.

Artists and creative people have long been captivated by the tranquillity and unspoilt beauty of the area. The artist Charles Lamb, RHA (1893-1964) lived and worked here for most of his life. One of the most spectacular man-made features in the district is the Open Air Sculpture Park, exhibiting the metal sculptures of Edward Delaney. Delaney's studio and home are close to the park. Admission to the exhibition is free of charge.

In 1891 the Congested Districts Board set up a knitting factory in the village, to give employment to women and girls. Bob Quinn took over the premises and turned it into a film studio. From this studio Quinn has produced many fine films including *Poitín*(1978), *The Bishop's Story* and *Buddawanny* (1986), based on the novel by Fr Pádraig Standún. *Poitín* was made with the involvement of local people in Connemara and traced the life of a poitín maker (Cyril Cusack) and his accomplices Donal McCann and Niall Tóibín. The film had Irish dialogue and

English sub-titles. In 1991 Bob Quinn's novel, *Smokey Hollow* was published.

Fr Pádraig Standún was born in the village of Belcarra near Castlebar in 1946. He became a priest and served on the Aran Islands and later in Carraroe but is now back in Inishmaan. His book *Suil le Breith* (filmed as *Budawanny*), was written in Irish. He has written other books in Irish and English including *Lovers* and *Celibates*.

The development of an industrial estate has added to employment and prosperity for Carraroe. In 1981 the hi-tech industry EFI, producing cables and harnesses for computers, opened a plant in the village and now employs 200 people.

Carraroe is a lively centre for holidays with beaches and walks to occupy the daytime hours and a variety of traditional music, set dancing and discos to add to the 'craic' at night.

RECOMMENDED

Óstan Cheathru Rua.
Coral Beach.
Coillean Caravan and Camping Park.
Angling.
Open Air Sculpture Park.
Óstan an Doilin.
Carraroe Holiday Village.

Lettermore

From Carraroe take the route northwards until you reach the T-junction and then bear left and follow the signpost for Lettermore. There is a series of islands situated between Kilkieran Bay and Casla Bay. The four largest of the islands, Eanach Mheáin, Lettermore, Gorumna and Lettermullen are connected to the mainland by a series of bridges which were erected at the end of the last century. The building of the bridges, causeways and roads was one of the most important projects of the Congested Districts Board. The work was designed by Colonel Peacocke and the contractor for most of the work was Patrick Toole of Lettermore.

The islands lie off the main tourist trail but are well worth a visit. In recent years a group of people have formed a Tourism committee in an effort to entice more visitors to the islands. This is the most traditional part of the entire county and remains largely uncommercialised. In ancient times monks and holy men came to the islands for solitude. There are the remains of several churches and holy wells on the islands.

The area is part of the Connemara Gaeltacht and Irish is the spoken language. A nine hole golf course, surrounded by sea, is being constructed on Eanach Mheáin. There are only six inhabitants still living on Inis Treabhair and one man remaining on Inis Bearacháin, who regularly rows to the mainland for provisions.

Lettermore is a picturesque village situated in the middle of the island of the same name and is connected to the mainland by a bridge. The main road runs through the centre of the island, with minor roads running west and north. The name Lettermore in Irish is Leitir Móir (Big Wet Hillside). The landscape is blanketed by fields of stone, dotted by small lakes and the remains of giant pine stumps. The cottages are simple and neat and outside of each there is a reek of turf. In the Penal Days Lettermore was a garrisoned island and a special law was passed restricting the movement of priests and monks. On the eastern shore, four miles south of the bridge, at Trá Bán (White Strand), are the remains of a medieval church.

Ruairí Ó Conchubhair in his grocery shop in the village is extremely helpful with information for tourists. Deep sea angling trips can be organised from the islands. For the more energetic, bicycles can be hired locally. It is ideal terrain for exploring on foot. In August 1993 Lettermore gained national prominence, when a local woman won over £3 million in the National Lottery, the highest single cash prize ever.

Gorumna Island is situated to the south of Lettermore, to which it is connected by a road bridge. The name of this, the largest of the islands, in Irish is Oileán Garomna (possibly meaning Headland). In 1888

Tiernea National School was built on the island and in 1949 it was replaced by a more modern building. There is an Údaras na Gaeltachta complex of small industries on Gorumna. Beside the complex there is a Heritage Centre which is worth a visit to view the exhibition and photographs of the island's past. There is also a Tourist Office and coffee shop which open during the summer months. The island has several safe beaches which are suitable for swimming.

For decades it has been strongly believed that poteen, the illicit whiskey, was secretly distilled on the islands. Frequently the gardai have raided suspect areas and destroyed the stills. In 1977 gardai raided a major still on Gorumna and poured the contents into the lake.

Due west from Gorumna is Lettermullen, the last and most westerly of the islands. The name in Irish is Leitir Mealláin, (Meallan's Wet Hillside). South of the bridge there is the ruin of an old castle built by Murrough Mac Hugh in the sixteenth century. Nearby, are the remains of a plain ancient church. Beyond the south-west corner of the island, a Signal Tower was erected on Golam Head in 1804, as a watch tower. From the late nineteenth century turf deposits on the island had been dug out and the locals had to carry their supplies four miles from Gorumna.

Travellers should drive as far as the road will take them, stop and walk to the western shore. From here there is a great view of some of the smaller islands off the coast.

RECOMMENDED

Heritage Centre.
Tourist Office.
Martello Tower.
Old castle.
Beaches.
Island Holiday Cottages.
The Hooker Bar.
Golf Course.
Bicycle Hire.
Deep sea angling.

Screeb

From Lettermore travellers should retrace their tracks across the islands back to the mainland and follow the signpost to Costelloe. There they will take a northerly direction to the small village of Screeb. The name Screeb in Irish is Scríob (Track). The district around Screeb is surrounded by a wild beauty of bog and lakes which are noted for their excellent fishing. Recently on a lake bordering the road I counted up to fifty swans gliding gracefully.

Part of the new road network, constructed by Alexander Nimmo, extends from the old iron works to Screeb Bridge. The road westwards from Screeb Lodge runs close to Camus Bay. In 1839 Thomas Fuge, acquired land from the Lynches of Barna and eight years later he built Screeb Lodge. Early in the twentieth century the building and adjoining land came into the ownership of the St Georges of Tyrone. They planted pine trees on the estate. A later resident of Screeb Lodge was Lord Dudley, Lord Lieutenant of Ireland. His wife, who initiated a nursing scheme to supply nurses to the deprived areas of Connemara, was drowned near the lodge in 1920.

RECOMMENDED

Screeb Lodge Restaurant.

Today Screeb Lodge House is an ideal location for those seeking accommodation or a first class restaurant, with easy access to prime fishing.

Rosmuc

At Screeb take the road west and after about three miles you will reach Lough Aroolagh and Gortmore. Rosmuc (or Rosmuck) in Irish is Ros Muc (Headland of Pigs) is also the name of a small village at the south end of the peninsula of Rosmuc.

In the townland of Turlough is the cottage which Pádraig Pearse used as a summer home. Pearse, poet and author, was commander of the Dublin insurgents in the GPO (General Post Office), at Easter 1916. His writings in Irish and English drew much inspiration from the people and surrounding countryside. While in Rosmuc he wrote most of his works, including the O'Donovan Rossa graveside oration which he delivered in Glasnevin Cemetery in 1915. The cottage beside a small lake, noted for its brown trout, is now a national monument. It is open to the public each summer.

RECOMMENDED

Pearse's Cottage.
Old Cemetery.
Séipéal an Ioncolnaithe.
Rosmuc Knitwear.
Connemara Marble.
Tí Clarke's Pub.
Seoid Marble Crafts.

In September 1920 during the War of Independence Rosmuc became the centre for one of the four Battalions of the Irish Volunteers, organised in Connemara under Colm Ó'Gaora. In April 1921 the Volunteers ambushed an RIC patrol between Rosmuc and Screeb, wounding one constable and capturing two revolvers and one rifle. Later the Black and Tans burned Pearse's cottage and several others in the area.

There are a number of craft centres in the district including Rosmuc Knitwear, Seoid Marble Crafts and Connemara Marble. A lively atmosphere can be experienced in Tí Clarke's Pub. The former home of Irish writer Pádraic Ó Conaire is to become a residential Arts Centre for artists working through the Irish language.

Below: Pádraig Pearse's Cottage

Kilkieran

From Rosmuc return to the junction at Gortmore and continue left to the next intersection where you turn left again and follow the coastal route to Kilkieran. This is a small coastal village, situated between the sea and the hills. The name in Irish is Cill Chiaráin (St Kieran's Church). St Kieran is believed to have landed here on his journey to the Aran Islands. St Kieran's Bay is named after the saint. St Kieran's Well is in the hilly cemetery and there is an annual pilgrimage to it on 9 September.

Two good stopping points in the village are Keane's Bar and Peter O'Grady's pub for a drink and a sing-song. The sea and fishing are important features around Kilkieran. There is excellent salmon and lobster fishing at Carna.

In 1949 the Government financially boosted the seaweed industry providing badly needed employment in the area. For many generations people used to gather seaweed along the coastline to fertilise the soil. Seaweed is still harvested, treated and exported for use in a variety of food and beverage products.

West of Kilkieran Bay is the parish of Moyrus, where according to James Hardiman, the historian, an abbot of a Cistercian Monastery in Donegal sought refuge for many years, as the English had put a price on his head.

Kilkieran is a Gaeltacht area with Irish an everyday spoken language. Students come from throughout the country to attend courses, and various sporting and cultural events, all through the medium of Irish. Most of the activities take place in the new community centre which has squash courts, games rooms, volleyball and tennis courts. Students live in the homes of local families.

There are many safe and sandy beaches in the locality. The harbour offers sheltered mooring for small vessels. Currach racing is a popular event during the summer months.

RECOMMENDED

Keane's Bar.
O'Grady's Pub.
Harbour.
Beaches.

Carna

Five miles south-west of Kilkieran is the small village of Carna situated in a secluded inlet to the extreme west of the Connemara Gaeltacht. The name Carna, which is the same in Irish means, 'a Sepulchral pile of Stones.' This is another sea-faring district with many locals making their living from fishing and the lobster fishing centre.

Carna comes alive each July with Féile Mhic Dara, a three day festival, featuring currach and hooker racing, sea angling competitions and traditional music. Boats can be hired here for visitors to travel to MacDara's Island. There is an abundance of ceilí and traditional music sessions during the tourist season. An interesting feature of this part of the country is the mobile bank which visits the village weekly.

Legend has it, that when St Patrick visited Carna he enquired from a 'wise woman' how old she was. She replied that she never slept when she was tired and when she walked she would wash her feet. Again he asked her how old she was and she replied that she was unsure but every year she threw a bone up on the roof. St Patrick put a young boy up there to count them and he is still counting them.

In the early nineteenth century the British feared an invasion of Ireland by Napoleonic forces and they built a series of Signal towers around the coast. One of these was at Cuilleen Hill, near Carna. In 1820, with the improvement of the road network throughout Connemara by Alexander Nimmo, a new road was extended south to Carna.

In 1880 the Sisters of Mercy opened a convent in the village. The area suffered greatly from famine and poverty and many families were forced to emigrate. So great were the numbers wishing to emigrate that the local clergy had to make the selection. In June 1880 Fr Greally, Parish Priest of Carna, chose ten families, averaging nine members to each family and escorted them to Galway docks, where they were provided with passage money to transport them by steamer to America.

In 1881 the Sisters of the Order of Mercy opened a school in Carna. The Congested Districts Board (1891-1923) provided teachers and also gave assistance and advice in the purchase of materials and in the sale of the girls' work. The Board gave instructions in the building and repairing of boats to local boat-wrights to encourage growth in the fishing industry. The Board also made a grant of £400 to the Carna Industries Association, to help create home industries.

In 1921, during the War of Independence, four Volunteers of the Third Battalion left Carna by boat to sail to their headquarters in Roundstone but they never reached their destination. Shooting was heard off the coast and it is believed that someone informed on them, resulting in their deaths. In November of that year the RIC barracks in

Carna was closed.

St MacDara's Island (Oileán Mhic Dara) due west of Carna, is one of the many uninhabited islands off the coast of Connemara. On the eastern shore of the sixty acre island is the Church of St MacDara which was founded in the sixth century by St MacDara, as a place of solitude. The original church was a wooden structure. St MacDara, who is buried on the island, is still honoured by the people of the district and on his feast day, 16 July, people make their way to the island for a special mass. When sailing boats were active the fishermen used to dip their sails three times on passing the island. The stone roof of the church was recently restored.

The traveller should make a detour three miles south of Carna to Mweenish, an island, connected to the mainland by a bridge.

In 1960 an Irish college was established in Carna where students can learn Irish during the summer months. Some of the families house up to a dozen students in their home at any one time, gaining extra revenue for themselves during the summer months. The summer also finds the hotel and pubs providing traditional music sessions and ceilis. There is a lively weekend of sean-nós (old style) singing every Whit and a more traditional festival can be enjoyed by tourists and locals each July.

In 1993 a fire destroyed the local Gaelic Seafood factory, which was mainly involved in salmon fishing.

RECOMMENDED

Sceirde House Hotel.
Mac's Bar and Hostel.
Tig Moráin.
St MacDara's Island.
Féile Mhic Dara (July).
Joe Heaney Weekend for sean-nós singing (Whit Weekend).

Below: Connemara landscape near Carna

Cashel

The drive from Carna to Cashel should be taken at a leisurely pace as it offers some of the most spectacular coastal scenery in Ireland, combining lakes, mountains and seascapes.

Cashel is a small attractive village situated on Cashel Bay, an inlet of Bertraghboy Bay. Cashel, An Caiseal (an ancient round mortarless stone fort), takes its name from the ancient ringfort-type burial ground on a hill about a mile north-east of the village. Near the burial ground is Toberconnell, St Conall's Well. About three miles west of Cashel is Toombeola Bridge, near which are the remains of a Dominican Abbey, founded in 1427 by one of the O'Flahertys who were dominant in Connemara for many centuries.

In 1847, with the outbreak of famine, Daniel Bowden Smith, a local landlord opened a food kitchen, at his own expense, close to Cashel. Four years later he became ill and died.

In April 1922 following the War of Independence a large Pro-Treaty meeting was held in Cashel. There are two first class hotels in Cashel, The Cashel House Hotel and the Zetland Hotel. In 1969 President Charles de Gaulle of France and his wife spent a holiday in the Cashel House Hotel. Local folklore has it a specific bed had to be made for the President as he was so tall. His visit and the ensuing favourable publicity brought a subsequent rise in the number of French tourists visiting the country. The hotel is still noted for its afternoon teas.

Cashel is another good shooting, angling and fishing centre. Boats are for hire locally. The Cashel Equestrian Centre welcomes visitors. Take the mountain track to view Connemara at its best. The traveller should also pay a visit to the Connemara Marble Studio.

RECOMMENDED

Cashel Equestrian Centre.
Cashel House Hotel.
Connemara Marble Studio.
Zetland Hotel.
Glynsk House Hotel.

Recess

From Cashel take a northerly direction and follow the signpost for Recess. The name Recess in Irish is Sraith Salach (Fenland of Willows), which would appear to be named after an area in the locality. Recess is a long sprawling village running alongside a lake, with the church, school and a shopping complex several miles apart. An unusual feature of the village is the Mexican-style St Patrick's Catholic Church. The village is situated on the main Galway to Clifden road.

From the 1820s the Martin family quarried green Connemara marble in the vicinity. There was a short revival of the industry here in the 1960s but it has since ceased. In the mid-1840s William Andrews, an Alderman from Dublin, rented an estate in the area. Within a decade Andrews had developed the residence into a hotel.

In 1895 a railway station and hotel opened in Recess, following the inception of the Galway to Clifden line. Ninety-six men were employed on constructing this stretch of the line, which was a difficult undertaking as they had to cut through a large hill. In 1903 King Edward VII and Queen Alexandra paid a visit to Recess and were greeted by a large crowd, including forty men riding bareback Connemara ponies. The royal party boarded a special train for Galway.

When the War of Independence ended in 1921 and an Anglo-Irish Treaty was established many Volunteers on the run came down from the mountains into Recess. In October 1922 the Recess Hotel, owned by the Midland Great Western Railway Company, was occupied by Republicans and destroyed by fire. The staff were given time to evacuate the building before it was torched. Recess Railway Station is now Caher House Restaurant.

The climb up Lissoughter Mountain, 1314 feet, is worth the effort for the view it affords of the wood, Glendalough Lake and Lough Inagh. Another worthwhile stop is at the shopping complex. Opposite the shops there is a Connemara Marble sculpture, overlooking the lake. The name Joyce is quite prominent in the locality. On the list of altar servers in the Catholic church I counted five Joyces among the nine names.

RECOMMENDED

Caher House Restaurant.
St Patrick's Church.
Glendalough House Pitch and Putt.
Lough Inagh Lodge.
Joyce's Craft Shop.
Glendalough House.
Glendalough Lake.
Connemara Marble Sculpture.
Inagh Valley Inn.
Paddy Festy's Pub.
Lissoughter Mountain.

RECESS

Oughterard

Oughterard is a charming, small village, approximately seventeen miles from Galway on the main Galway to Clifden Road. The village, known in Irish as Úachtar Árd (the Higher Upper Place), is strategically placed on the Owenriff River. The area, often referred to as 'the Gateway to Connemara', is noted for its excellent salmon and trout angling on the river and nearby Lough Corrib. Fishermen from throughout Europe have been enjoying the prime fishing here for over 150 years. Oughterard is the most convenient centre for those wishing to fish on Lough Corrib. There are many outlets in the village to purchase fishing tackle and supplies.

There is great craic in the pubs and hotels each night as foreigners and locals exchange tall tales on 'the one that got away.' Other forms of relaxation in the vicinity can be enjoyed at Oughterard 18 Hole Golf Club or by merely cruising on the lake. There are many first class hotels in easy range of the village including Connemara Gateway Hotel, Corrib Hotel, Sweeney's Hotel and Ross Lake House Hotel.

At the end of the fifteenth century the Burkes built a castle at Aughnanure, two miles east of Oughterard. The castle, with a six storey tower, stands on an island of rocks surrounded by a fast stream. The castle was later taken over by the O'Flaherty family, who were the scourge of Galway city. In 1488 Oughterard was transferred to the wardenship of Galway by William Joyce. In 1572 Sir Edward Fitton attacked Aughnanure Castle but was withheld by the O'Flahertys. In 1618 King James I granted the castle to Hugh O'Flaherty. In 1652, during the Cromwellian blockade of Galway, Aughnanure Castle was one of the outposts which guarded the city from attack at the head of the lake. David Duignan, unperturbed by the attacks, was in the castle compiling a manuscript (now in the possession of the Royal Irish Academy). Following the fall of Galway, Cromwellian troops headed west through Oughterard and over the bogs of Connemara to quell the last outposts of resistance in Cleggan and Inishbofin. In recent years the castle has been restored and is now open to the public.

In the 1830s there was an active spa in the village. Within a decade, with the outbreak of famine, there was extensive poverty in the district. Lord Wainright, a local landlord, on seeing the plight of the people issued food free to them. To further ease the conditions of the poor, a workhouse was built in the village.

There was speculation that the Galway to Clifden railway line would take the coastal route through Spiddal but a Royal Commission decided on a route through Oughterard. In 1862 the line from Galway reached Oughterard and there were appeals to the railway company to continue

Above and left: Aughnanure Castle

the line to Clifden. That opened in 1895.

On 23 April 1922 following the War of Independence (1919-1921), Eamon de Valera spoke at a large Anti-Treaty meeting held in Oughterard Market Square. On the night of 25 July 1922 Republican forces burned the police station and workhouse. They were strongly condemned by the clergy for their action. By October 1922 the Free State troops had entered Oughterard and efforts were made to regain the railway line. In December Republicans made attacks on military posts around Oughterard.

A number of prominent people have had connections with Oughterard. In 1833 Maria Edgeworth set out from the village by coach to visit Ballynahinch Castle. In 1890 Edith Somerville and Violet Martin stayed in the village before commencing a tour of Connemara. In 1912 James Joyce and Nora Barnacle cycled to Oughterard from Galway. Walter Macken, the actor, author and playwright, and his family lived close to the village from 1951-65. He did much of his writing here and was a popular figure in the community. According to his son Ultan, Walter's daily routine was that he would attend eight o'clock mass, return home to have his breakfast and read the paper. At ten o'clock he would walk around his study, smoking, for an hour, before starting to write. The American actress, Barbara Bel Geddes, best known as Miss Ellie in *Dallas*, the television series, lived for a period near the village.

Close to the village is the small medieval church of Kilcummin and St Cummin's Well. A road north from the village will take travellers to the shore of Lough Corrib where they will have an excellent view of Inchagoill (Inis an Ghaill, Island of the Stranger), the largest island on the lake. On the island there is the fifth century church of Tempall Phádraig. On the south-east side is Teampall na Naomh (Church of the Saints) which dates to the ninth century. Other interesting features of the island are the obelisk, bearing Roman characters, and the Stone of Lugna, who is believed to have been the nephew and the navigator of St Patrick. The island may be reached by boat from Oughterard.

RECOMMENDED

Aughnanure Castle.
Oughterard Golf Club.
Lough Corrib Hostel.
Sweeney's Hotel.
Queen of Connemara Festival (July).
Connemara Gateway Hotel.
Lough Corrib.
Corrib Hotel.
Monahan's Craft and Coffee Shop.
Fuschia Crafts.

Moycullen

From Oughterard continue south-east towards Galway until you reach the small village of Moycullen, which is ideally located for exploring Connemara and the Corrib Country. The name Moycullen in Irish is Mag-Uillín (The Plains of Uillin), and according to *A Dictionary of Irish Place-Names* by Adrian Room, the name is Maigh Cuilinn (Plain of Holly). There is a local legend that, during the period of the Tuatha Dé Danann, a fight developed between the leader of the Tuatha Dé Danann, Orbsen Mac Alloid and Uillínn, grandson of Wuada of the Silver Head, against a King of Ireland on the western shores of Lough Corrib near Moycullen. It is believed that Moycullen derived its name from this fight.

In 1488 William Joyce was granted the Wardenship of Moycullen. The eastern faction of the O'Flaherty tribe ruled from Moycullen towards Galway. The Barony of Moycullen was created in 1585 from the two ancient territories of Gnomore and Gnobeg. Mc Conraoi was chief of Gnomore and O'Heyny was chief of Gnobeg.

The Connemara Marble Factory and Shop are worth a visit by souvenir hunters. Connemara marble which is quarried close to the village is cut into ornaments and bracelets at the factory. There are several craft and coffee shops in Moycullen and its environs. The area also has a good choice of pubs and restaurants. For those wishing to experience a gourmet meal, the internationally award winning Drimcong House Restaurant is a must. On the Moycullen Road there are many locations where the traveller will have elevated views of Lough Corrib.

In 1655 transportation (the punishment of sending prisoners to a penal colony overseas) commenced and the order 'To Hell or Connacht' became a familiar cry. Ulster families were forced to leave their homes and settle in Moycullen and other designated parts of Connacht. They experienced a difficult task as they journeyed westwards. Following death, starvation, imprisonment and transportation the area was depopulated and Cromwellian troops were granted land and houses in lieu of wages.

In the seventeenth century the O'Flahertys built a castle in Moycullen which was purchased from them by the Martin family. In 1660 Richard Martin, known as 'Nimble Dick', changed his allegiance from King James II to King William and was granted the O'Flaherty lands in Connacht and acquired the Barony of Moycullen. Major Poppleton, husband of one of the Martin women, lived here following his dismissal from his position as one of Napoleon's protectors on St Helena, for, allegedly, having been too friendly towards Napoleon. He is buried in the family tomb at Ross.

Four miles from the village is the square bulk of Ross House or Castle which was the home of the Martin family who went bankrupt during the famine. Violet Martin, later to gain fame as Martin Ross, was born here in 1861. She collaborated with her cousin, Edith Somerville, in their series of Somerville and Ross novels and stories. Their best known works were *The Real Charlotte* and *The Reminiscences of an Irish RM*, which was turned into a popular television series. Nearby Ross Lake is noted for its coarse fishing.

East of Lough Lonan is St Annin's Well. Close by was the medieval parish church of Killannin. Only the ruins survive today.

Elizabeth, countess of Fingal, was born at Danesfield House, near the village. Her book, *Seventy Years Young*, gave a sharp insight into Anglo-Irish Society in the Victorian-Edwardian era (mid nineteenth century to early twentieth century).

When the Galway to Clifden railway line was operating, Moycullen had a station with a goods store and a hundred foot long platform. Many passengers alighted here to fish on Lough Corrib. During the War of Independence, British troops were stationed in Moycullen and, on several occasions, the Volunteers sabotaged the line to prevent the transportation of troops and supplies. In October 1922 Free State troops entered the village and efforts were made to repair the line. In December 1922 Republican troops attacked the village.

Left: 'Nimble Dick'

RECOMMENDED

Drimcong House.
Restaurant.
Ross House.
White Gables Restaurant.
Cloonabinnia House Hotel.
Celtic Crystal.
Craft and Antique Shop.
Connemara Marble Factory and Shop.
Church of the Immaculate Conception.

North Connemara

For the tour of North Connemara I will begin at Maam Cross and travel in an anti-clockwise direction. In the main, the inhabited districts are situated along the coastline. The route is a leisurely drive with stopping points for a drink, snack or gourmet meal. It is a stiff cycle and not for the uninitiated, although it can be tackled over a number of days with overnight stops in a variety of hostels, lodges and guesthouses. Pack rain gear, as all four seasons can be experienced in a single day. The ever changing skies offer a challenge for painters and photographers and there is an abundance of lakes, rivers and beaches for anglers to choose from. The natural unspoilt terrain and unpolluted waters should gladden the heart of any environmentalist.

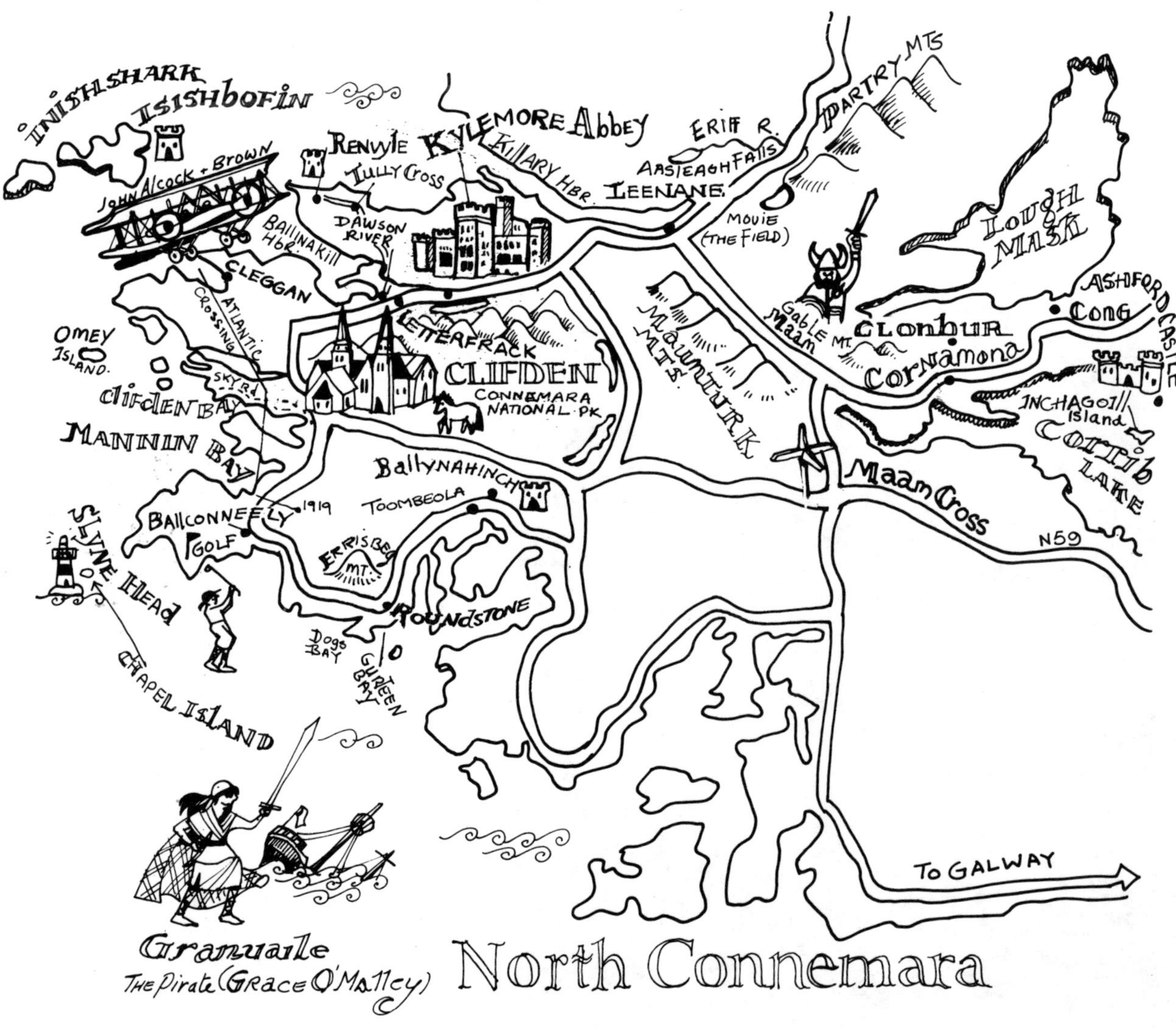

Maam Cross

Maam Cross is a location which almost every visitor to Connemara will encounter. The name applies to what is little more than a crossroads on the main Galway to Clifden road and divides north and south Connemara. At this juncture it is advisable to stop and consult the array of signposts or a road map. Maam Cross in Irish is An Teach Dóite (The Burnt House). It is an excellent angling centre, surrounded by lakes, rivers, forests and bog. For the thirsty or hungry traveller, Peacocke's restaurant and bar is well worth checking out. In the bar there are regular screenings of the film, *The Quiet Man*, which was responsible for placing this area on the tourist map. Beside the restaurant is a replica thatched cottage, similar to the one featured in the film.

Traditionally Maam Cross has been the location of a monthly horse fair and the October horse fair still exists today. The fair creates a lively atmosphere as deals are struck and farmers and traders sell their livestock and wares.

In 1893 Maam Cross was to become an important stopping off place between Galway and Clifden when the Midland Great Western Railway Company opened a station there. The station had a cattle and goods platform. At the turn of the century many visitors travelled by train to paint, write and fish in the tranquillity of the area. Paul Henry, the artist who captured the changing skies and landscapes of Connemara so vividly on canvas, often used Maam Cross as a base for his painting expeditions. Pádraig Pearse frequently used this station when travelling from Dublin to his holiday home in Rosmuc. The railway continued to operate until 1930.

In 1920 a consignment of arms arrived at Maam Cross Station bound for the Volunteers and an unsuspecting British officer ordered his troops to transport them to an address in Leenane. In 1921 Volunteers burned the Barracks at Maam Cross. That same year the local Volunteers captured a British army patrol, close to Maam Cross and took their arms, wounding one soldier.

With a full tank or bicycle tyres pumped up, we will commence our tour of North Connemara by taking the road northwards towards the village of Maam.

RECOMMENDED

Peacocke's.
Thatched Cottage.
Old Railway Station.
October Horse Fair.

Maam

The five mile drive will take the traveller through windswept, breathtaking countryside, with lakes and bog on either side and the stark Leckavrea Mountain to the left. The word Maam derives from the Irish word Mám, meaning 'Mountain Pass', which is an accurate description of this small village at the head of the valley. Behind the village Lugnabrick Mountain rises to 1628 feet. The Joyce, Failmore and Bealanabrack rivers meet in the village and flow to connect with Lough Corrib.

Close to Maam, take a left hand turn to one of the main locations for the film *The Quiet Man*. In 1951, the distinguished American film director, John Ford, chose this picturesque setting to build John Wayne's cottage in the film. Today only the ruins of the cottage remain but older locals will be only too pleased to recall tales of the making of this classic film.

This area is known as Joyce Country (Dúiche Sheoigheach) and lies between Connemara and County Mayo, east of Lough Corrib. The centre of Joyce Country extends from Maam Cross to Leenane, bordered by the Maamturk Mountains to the south-west, and by the Partry Mountains to the north. The Joyce family came to Galway from Wales in the thirteenth century and settled in the area, giving their name to this district of mountains, valleys and lakes.

In 1810 the engineer, Alexander Nimmo, built both the hotel and bridge in Maam. In a fierce flood the stone bridge was swept away and was later replaced by an iron structure. Nimmo used the hotel as a residence and pay office during the construction of bridges, roads and piers throughout Connacht. The hotel later became a Bianconi posting inn and was one of the oldest licensed premises in Ireland.

Later Nimmo constructed the harbour in Galway and designed a canal from there to Lough Corrib. In 1824 an Act of Parliament was passed to make Lough Corrib navigable from Galway to Maam via Oughterard. Work commenced on the project in 1850 and the service, which cost £102,289, opened in 1859. The service ran three days a week. The fare was 2*s*. 6*d*. first class, and 6*d*. second class. In 1862 the Eglington, an iron boat, began a regular service. As there was little development of road transport in the area, the steamer carried both passengers and cargo. The Galway to Clifden railway line, completed in 1893, took away a significant amount of this traffic. The service closed to commercial traffic in 1930.

During the War of Independence in April 1921, when an attempt was made by the British forces to round up the Connemara Volunteers, the rebels sought refuge in a house near Maam. The RIC moved in but the Volunteers held them off, killing one RIC constable. Reinforcements of troops and RIC men arrived and set about burning them out but the

Volunteers escaped into the mountains. During the IRA activity of 1921 many local men, including fishermen, were arrested and taken to Maam barracks on suspicion of being members of the organisation. The owner of the Leenane Hotel spoke up on their behalf and they were released.

On coming to the T-junction in the village, the traveller will reach Keane's Bar and the adjoining Keane's Hardware and Supermarket which stocks practically everything.

A jetty at Maam Bridge gives direct access by river to Lough Corrib. Three miles west of the village is Kilmilkin Catholic Church, which has a stained glass window by Evie Hone and is well worth viewing.

On leaving Maam on the road to Cornamona, you'll catch a glimpse of Hen Castle, also known as Castle Kirke on Lough Corrib. According to legend, a witch and her hen built the castle in one night. The witch gave the castle to one of the O'Flahertys stating, that if he was ever attacked, the hen would lay enough eggs to feed him. When the castle was besieged, O'Flaherty ate the hen and had to surrender due to lack of food. In reality, according to the *Annals of the Four Masters*, the castle was built in 1226 by Richard de Burgo and the sons of Roderick O'Connor. In 1256, Walter de Burgo, first Earl of Ulster, marched against Roderick O'Connor and took possession of Lough Corrib and fortified Castle Kirke.

RECOMMENDED

Keane's Pub & Hardware Shop.
Mountain walks.
Old Court House.
Kilmilkin Catholic Church.
The Quiet Man Cottage.
Saint Patrick's Well.
Maam County Knitwear.

Below: Derryclare Lake

Cornamona

At Maam the traveller should make a short detour by turning right and continuing on to the small village of Cornamona. The five mile drive offers some of the finest views of Lough Corrib. There are a number of pull-ins, where the lake can be viewed from an elevated level. The name in Irish is Corr Na Móna (Round Hill of the Bog). The small village is situated on the north-west shore of Lough Corrib on Doorus Peninsula and is divided by the Dooghta River. The lake and river are eagerly sought out by anglers as they afford some of the best salmon and trout fishing in the county. There are three public rights-of-way to Lough Corrib and some signposted scenic walks which are recommended. It is worth driving, cycling or walking down Doorus Peninsula where there are many excellent fishing locations.

Beside the road from Maam to Clonbur are lead mines, which are now closed. When the mines were in operation, early this century, the minerals were transferred by steamer down Lough Corrib to Galway.

Cornamona is one of the most popular Gaeltacht districts in North Connemara and Irish is the every day language of many people. The Irish summer college, Coláiste Dhúiche Sheoigheach, offers intensive Irish courses for students, aged 10-18 from June to August. There is a vibrant community spirit and a community co-operative of small industries. A large number of people are involved in the tourist industry. A range of guesthouses offer accommodation and angling along with boating facilities.

To the north of Cornamona is Mount Gable Mountain, where, according to legend, the Fir Bolg gathered on the summit before encountering the Tuatha Dé Danann in the Battle of Moytura. Later the isthmus was named the Gap of Danger (Bearna Baoil) where the O'Flaherty and Joyce clans withstood attacks by raiders from the east. Mount Gable is not a difficult climb but worth the effort for the panoramic view.

Stories of the day's catches or 'the escapee,' can be exchanged at music sessions in O'Malleys or Cohan's Pub. For those interested in the local history, the proprietor of the Galway Woollen Market is an authority on the subject. Each March there is an Irish Drama Festival in the village.

RECOMMENDED

Salmon Smokery.
O'Malley's Pub.
Galway Woollen Market.
Cohan's Pub.
Tennis Court.
Colaiste Dhúiche Sheoigheach.
18 Hole Pitch and Putt.
Mount Gable.
Irish Drama Festival (March).

Above and left: Scenes from 'The Quiet Man' with John Wayne and Barry Fitzgerald

Clonbur

The village of Clonbur lies between Lough Corrib and Lough Mask, close to the County Mayo border. The name in Irish is Fairche (Diocese). The village was originally called Fairhill, after the Fair family. William Fair was a tutor to the Kildare family. Fair fell in love with one of Kildare's daughters. They eloped and settled in Clonbur. Years later when their son became Lord Leitrim's agent and a wealthy man, he named the place Fairhill.

Clonbur has changed little in the intervening years. Kynes shop will supply the visitor with anything from information, to fishing tackle to groceries. The Forestry and Wildlife Service has begun creating forest trails and there are leaflets of suggested walks available.

South of the village are magnificent views of Lough Corrib. The beauty of the area was noted by Sir William Wilde in 1867 in his book *Lough Corrib*: 'Steal in among the West Connacht, Joyce Country, and Connemara ranges — the Jura and the Alps of Ireland — and give fitful atmospheric changes to the colourings of the landscape. From bright early dawn to sombre eve, scenes of beauty and sublimity are presented that leave us nothing to envy, even in the everlasting snowtops with their vine-clad slopes and dark pine-robed sides, the mighty glaciers, the rushing avalanches, nor the deep ultramarine skies of other lands.'

Sir Henry Lynch, a Galway Catholic MP, had his estate in Galway confiscated by Cromwell's force in 1659 and in 1678 his son, Maurice Lynch, obtained under an act of settlement 'two quarters of land in Ballynoonagh Clonbur'. Maurice's grandson, also named Maurice, was the first Lynch to reside in Ballynoonagh Castle. His son, Peter Lynch was knighted by the Pope while serving as a merchant in Gibraltar. In the 1760s on the death of his father he returned to Clonbur and built Petersburg House from the stone of Ballynoonagh after a fire had destroyed the castle. Petersburg Estate was to become one of the main seats of the Lynch family. One of the family, Thomas Lynch, was the youngest signatory of the American Declaration of Independence. Galway VEC (Vocational Education Committee) promotes an Outdoor Educational Centre at Petersburg House, where many water sports are taught.

There are numerous historical sites in the district. Close to the village is Ross Hill Abbey or Teampall Bhreandáin which dates back to the eighth century. The island of Inchagoill (the Island of the Strangers) on Lough Corrib is rich in history and folklore. There is a fifth century inscribed cross, reputed to be the earliest inscription in Ireland. The island's two churches have associations with Saint Patrick. A boat service runs to the island from Ashford Castle during the summer.

From Clonbur retrace your steps through Maam and follow the winding scenic route running parallel to the Joyce River.

RECOMMENDED

Tig de Burca Irish Pub.
Joyce and Rogan Bar.
Fairhill House Restaurant.
Ross Hill Abbey.
Forest Walks.
Petersburg Outdoor Educational Centre.
Inchagoill Island.
Ashford Castle.

Leenane

Approaching Clifden from the Westport Road, the first village the traveller will reach, just inside the northern boundary of County Galway, is Leenane. This is a small sheltered hamlet at the south-east corner of Killary Harbour, a narrow fjord-type formation. The name translates as An Líonán (the Shallow Sea-bed). The village is an ideal centre for fishing, shooting, walking and touring the Joyce Country. Leenane, once a station for the British Atlantic fleet, stands at the west end of the Partry mountains, dominated by the Devil's Mother, around which there have been many legends.

Nearby, on the border of County Mayo, the Eriff River tumbles over Aasleagh Falls, which are noted for their salmon and trout. There is a spectacular view from the bridge, particularly when the river is in flood. The state has acquired the river on behalf of the Central Fisheries Board.

In 1814 Alexander Nimmo, the Scottish civil engineer, recommended that a new network of roads should be constructed to form better communication between Connemara and County Mayo. Against the advice of local people he built a bridge and causeway across Killary Bay, which collapsed some years later.

In 1878 Oscar Wilde stayed for a time in Illaunroe Lodge, near the village. Close by is Rosroe Cottage which was rented by the artist Paul Henry, while he painted many of his Connemara landscapes. Early in the nineteenth century the Leenane Hotel was opened by Big Jack Joyce, a colourful character who entertained his guests. Later Major McKeown became an important landlord in the area, owning 100,000 acres, the Leenane Hotel, the post office and a shop. On 29 July 1903 he became extremely disgruntled when the royal yacht anchored in the bay and King Edward VII and the royal party drove in a carriage along the coast road but did not stop at Leenane.

In September 1920 Tom O'Malley organised the Third Battalion of the Irish Volunteers in Connemara, based in Leenane. On 23 April 1921 a patrol of 14 RIC men, under the command of Inspector Sugrue, set out from Oughterard and went on patrol near Leenane. As they approached the home of Pádraic O'Maille MP, they were ambushed and Constable Boylan, an RIC man, was shot dead in the exchange. Soon afterwards British navy gunboats sailed up Killary Bay to seek out pockets of resistance. Early in July 1921 a lorry load of British troops arrived in Leenane and many villagers, fearing arrest and the burning of their homes, sought refuge in the mountains.

In 1989, film director, Jim Sheridan, chose Leenane as the main location for his screen adaptation of John B Keane's *The Field*, a drama of lust for land. For two months the village played host to the film-makers,

RECOMMENDED

Leenane Cultural Centre and Restaurant.
Youth Hostel.
Holy Well.
Sheep and Wool Festival (Mid June).
Portfinn Seafood Restaurant.
The Field Coffee Shop.
Gaynor's 'The Field' Bar.
Killary Crafts.
Glen Valley Stables.
Hamilton's Pub.
Bay View House.
Glen Valley Farmhouse.

headed by Richard Harris, Tom Berenger, John Hurt and Brenda Fricker. Harris received an Academy Award nomination for his powerful portrayal of the farmer, Bull McCabe. Many locals were employed as extras on the film. Since the release of the film, some premises in the village have incorporated the title *The Field* into their name. Visitors to Gaynor's Pub can take a pint as they observe one of the main settings in the film and view many photographs and souvenirs of the production.

A welcome new addition to Leenane is the Cultural Centre and Restaurant. This Interpretive Centre exhibits the history and traditions of the sheep and wool industry in Ireland. Leenane is recommended for those seeking outdoor pursuits, with two adventure centres, pony trekking, shooting of woodcock, grouse and pheasant from November and fishing in the vicinity.

The Church of Our Lady of the Wayside, close to Leenane, is a bizarre shape and resembles a tent. Pattern day is 15 August, when there is an open market in the village.

John Hurt, Richard Harris and Sean Bean in a scene from 'The Field'

Kylemore

Following an interesting drive westward, along the Killary Fjord, the traveller will reach the Kylemore valley which lies between the Twelve Bens in the south and the wooded, 1736 foot Doughruagh Mountain to the north. Kylemore (An Choill Mhóir, the Big Wood) is a picturesque area, approached from the Inagh Valley, in North Connemara. From Kylemore Lough the Dawros River flows through the pass to Ballynakill Harbour. Three lakes, the Kylemore, the Top Lake and Castle Lake, bordered by rhododendrons, and crossed by the roadway, lie along the Dawros River. Kylemore Lake is about a mile long and runs alongside the road. It is a good angling centre with first class salmon and trout fishing.

In the seventeenth century the Darcy family settled in Kylemore. They were a benevolent family and built a workhouse to give shelter and relief to the poor in the district. Following the French landing in 1798 and the Battle of Ballinamuck, several of the United Irishmen sought refuge in the area. Johnny Gibbons, one of the rebels, took shelter in a cave on the mountain. He was later hanged in Westport, Co. Mayo. Between 1835-39 a Catholic chapel was built in Kylemore, southwest of the lake. From the mid-1840s it became fashionable for the English gentry to purchase land in the district.

In 1862 Mitchel Henry, a wealthy Liverpool merchant, inherited a fortune from his father with which he decided to build the Victorian Kylemore Castle. Two years later work commenced on the castle, to a design by Ussher Roberts and John F Fuller. The building was constructed in granite and limestone, at the foot of the steep Doughruagh, on the north shore of Pollacappul Lough. While building the castle, Mitchel Henry hired about a hundred labourers who walked to the site from the surrounding villages. Italian experts worked on the ornate ceiling. Henry demolished the small village of Polla in order to lay out gardens and reclaimed acres of bog on which he planted trees and shrubs. He also erected a small Gothic chapel with pillars of Connemara marble inside, and a chamber tomb nearby. Some of the Henry family were buried there. Mitchel Henry was elected MP for Galway.

In 1903 King Edward VII and Queen Alexandra visited Kylemore Castle where they enjoyed tea and a tour of the castle. Arches were erected on the route by locals to honour the royal couple. In 1920 the Benedictine nuns from Belgium (Irish Dames of Ypres) took over Kylemore Castle and opened it as a girls' secondary school for boarders and day pupils. For a period the sisters ran the castle as a hotel but a fire in January 1959 destroyed much of the building. The castle was rebuilt

RECOMMENDED

Kylemore Abbey.
Pass Inn Hotel.
Kylemore Craft Shop.
Many lodges which cater for fishing parties.

and reopened as a school. Later the sisters realised the tourist potential of the area and opened a craft shop, pottery showrooms and a restaurant beside the convent.

Kylemore Abbey Fishery covers the three lakes and about five miles of the Dawros River. At nearby Tagaillia is the site of a prehistoric chamber tomb.

In winter the area can be seen to best advantage with spectacular mini-waterfalls cascading down the mountainside. A note of caution: following heavy rain the traveller should be on the alert for serious flooding on many roads. For eager walkers a trail up behind the Abbey is recommended, for a splendid view of Kylemore Valley. In recent years with the increased business at the spin-off industries of the Abbey, a new car park and bridge have been constructed.

Kylemore Abbey (Michael Diggin)

Letterfrack

On leaving Kylemore continue westward on the main road towards Clifden until you reach the small village of Letterfrack. It is a lively junction and a variety of signposts will ensure that you are on the correct course. There are a number of brightly painted pubs and shops in the village which is the start of the Connemara National Park.

According to Weston St John Joyce, the name Letterfrack means Leitir-bhreac, Speckled Hillside or Sloping Field. Other sources give the translation as Leitir Fraic (Frac's Hillside).

In the mid-1840s there were over 500 people out of a population of 4808 in the auxiliary workhouse in Letterfrack. In 1847 James Ellis, a retired Quaker corn merchant and his wife Mary, from Bradford, England, settled in Letterfrack. They purchased 1800 acres, many of mountain and bog from the Graham family, the second largest landlords in the parish of Ballinakill. Ellis organised the building of a shop, several cottages and a large house for his family. He also opened a non-sectarian school and an orphanage. In 1855 a dispensary was set up by the Poor Law Guardians in a house beside the police barracks. During the famine, Ellis protected the people from its worse ravages and his wife gave food and clothes to the poor. Ellis established a basket-making industry which gave employment to women and girls. Later Sophie Sturge, a Quaker, took over and continued the business. Mr O'Grady, owner of Casson's Hotel, allowed her to use the annex of the hotel. The industry flourished and an export trade commenced.

In 1857 James Ellis became ill and sold the property to John Hall, of the Irish Church Missionary Society, for £3000. This was one of a number of mission centres established along the north Connemara coast. James Ellis returned to England, where he died in 1869.

CONNEMARA NATIONAL PARK

John Lydon worked for Francis Graham, the local landlord in Letterfrack. On the night of 24 April 1881 Lydon and his twenty year old son were dragged from their beds by a group of men and shot dead outside their cottage. A local man, Pat Walsh, was charged, tried and found guilty of their murders. He was executed in Galway Jail on 22 September 1881. On 15 February 1882 Constable Kavanagh, who was stationed at Letterfrack and gave evidence against Pat Walsh in his trial, was shot dead outside a pub. Michael Walsh, a brother of Pat's, was arrested and charged with the murder. He too was found guilty but the sentence was commuted to life imprisonment. The events became known as the Letterfrack Murders.

In April 1886 a certification was issued by Dublin Castle 'that St. Joseph's Industrial School for Roman Catholic Boys Letterfrack, was fit for the reception of male children, to be sent there under the Act of

Parliament of the Thirty-first year of the Reign of HM Queen Victoria.'

In the nineteenth century Archbishop McHale of Tuam purchased the Letterfrack estate and Christian Brothers under Brother Colman Flood opened an industrial school for delinquent boys. Discipline was severe. The school accommodated seventy-five boys which later increased to one hundred and fifty. In the workshops the boys were trained as bakers, tailors, shoemakers and carpenters. Clothes and footwear for the gentry were also manufactured by the boys. During the Second World War the school was self-sufficient with its own farm produce and it greatly eased conditions for the surrounding district. The Industrial School was closed in 1973.

In 1903 the royal couple, King Edward VII and Queen Alexandra, visited Letterfrack, during their tour of Connemara. 1905 saw the closing of the basket-making industry in the village and the factory was turned into a ballroom. In 1913 a receiver station was erected at Letterfrack for the Marconi station at Clifden. It communicated with a station in Canada. The operators lived in quarters at Derrygimlagh. After some years the station proved uneconomical and was closed. In 1922 the Letterfrack Volunteers, as was the case in many other parts of Connemara at the time, burned the local RIC barracks.

In 1980 the leading Swiss film director, Alain Tanner, came to Letterfrack to shoot an amazing film, *L 'Années Lumières*, (English title *Light Years Away*), a mystical fable set in the year 2000 and starring Trevor Howard and Mick Ford.

In 1978, Connemara West, a local community co-operative, acquired the industrial school and encouraged the development of small industries. Most of the Letterfrack estate was taken over by the Office of Public Works and opened as the Connemara National Park. There is a Visitors Centre, with an audio-visual theatre and information for tourists. During the summer season, fishing trips can be arranged locally and there are guided tours of places of interest. From Diamond Hill the traveller will have spectacular views of the surrounding countryside. The location is an artist's haven with 360° landscapes, surrounded by bog. Barnaderg Bay has good swimming with unspoilt beaches. For refreshments and night-time entertainment there are three pubs, Bard's Den, Veldon's and Molly's Pub at the crossroads. Roseleague Manor Hotel is to be recommended for a quiet, romantic break with excellent food.

RECOMMENDED

Connemara National Park.
Rosleague Manor Hotel.
Visitors' Centre.
Bard's Den Pub.
Vendon's Pub.
Molly's Pub.
Guided Tours (Summer months).
Old Monastery Hostel.
Sea Week (October).
Bog Week (end May).
Connemara Handcrafts.
Connemara Stoneworks.
Connemara West
Avoca Handweavers..

Left: Cross-leaved heather
(Irish Peatland Conservation Council)

Below: Connemara bog between Oughterard & Maam Cross (Michael Diggin)

Right : Bog cotton - a familiar sight in Connemara (Irish Peatland Conservation Council)

Galway hookers
in full sail (Nutan)

Tully / Tully Cross

At Letterfrack the traveller should take the right hand turn and travel northwards to the small twin villages of Tully and Tully Cross. The name Tully Cross in Irish is Crosaire an Tulaigh. Tully Cross has been given a traditional appearance by a number of thatched cottages. The rent-an-Irish-cottage scheme, built in the early 1970s was the first project of Connemara West, a community development company formed with the aim of encouraging the people to develop the area themselves. The cottages are available for renting all year round.

Locals from the community built the village of Tully in the late 1820s. For many years, up to the 1850s, there was no church in the district and locals had to attend mass in a house. Later, Henry Blake, the local landlord, donated land for the building of a church in Tully Cross. This was on the site of the present Church of Christ the King. The church is worth a visit to view Harry Clarke's fine three-light stained glass window. In the past the fair green was the setting for many cattle fairs and markets. The Renvyle Peninsula which extends west from Tully Cross, was once in the parish of Ballynakill which was established in 1585.

In 1913 the Tully Cross Corps of the Irish Volunteers was formed. On 4 September 1920 the local coastguard station was burned during an engagement.

In 1976 a Teach Ceoil (music house) was built in Tully, as a result of the rent-an-Irish-cottage project. This development led to the renewal of traditional music and culture in the area. Music sessions are held regularly in the hall during the summer months.

From May to September each year, this usually sleepy locality comes alive with an assortment of back-packers, Irish and European visitors and even Government ministers, escaping to recharge their batteries.

RECOMMENDED

Teach Ceoil.
Tourist Office (In Credit Union).
Anglers Rest Pub.
Derryglen Restaurant.
Christ the King Church.

Renvyle

From Tully Cross continue west-wards to the small coastal village of Renvyle. The name in Irish is Rinn Mhaoile (Bare Headland).

In the fourteenth century the O'Flahertys built Renvyle Castle (Rinn Mhil), overlooking the shore. In the early 1600s Murrough na Maor O'Flaherty, a great chief of the clan, purchased land from the O'Halloran family in Renvyle. On O'Flaherty's death in 1626 his son, Edmund, inherited the land and the castle. In 1546 Granuaile (Grace O'Malley) married Donal O'Flaherty and spent some time at the castle. In 1653 following the collapse of Inishbofin to Cromwellian troops, Edmund O'Flaherty, one of the islanders' defenders, went into hiding in the woods above Renvyle. He was captured, tried and executed. In 1680 the Renvyle estate was purchased by Henry Blake, a Protestant, from Richard, Earl of Westmeath. The Blakes were an old Galway family who acquired a large section of Connemara. At Renvyle they built an impressive house between the sea and the rocks.

In 1811 a ship was wrecked in a storm and its cargo of timber was washed up on the beach at Renvyle. In 1820 a girls' school was established under the auspices of the Kildare Place Society of Dublin. The school was controlled by the Blakes, although the pupils were Catholic. The school closed after four years. In the 1880s one of their descendants, Mrs Blake, a landlord, found herself in conflict with the Land League and her tenants, and she was forced to turn her house into a hotel. The writers Edith Somerville and Violet Martin stayed in the hotel during their tour of Connemara in 1890.

Early in the twentieth century Oliver St John Gogarty bought Renvyle House. Gogarty was an author, wit, physician and contemporary of James Joyce and the model for Buck Mulligan in *Ulysses*. W B Yeats visited the hotel and brought down the Abbey Theatre players to stage his play *The Hawk's Well*. While a guest at the hotel, Augustus John painted a portrait of W B Yeats. John Millington Synge also visited Gogarty and wrote fondly of the district. In February 1923 Renvyle House was attacked by Anti-Treaty forces because it was known that Gogarty supported the Free State side. In 1930, with the compensation, he rebuilt the building and opened it as a hotel. Today Renvyle House still trades as a hotel.

A reminder of the legend of *Diarmúid agus Gráinne* is to be found close to Renvyle at Ardnagreevagh, with a megalithic tomb called 'Diarmúid and Gráinne's bed'. Near Renvyle there is also the Gothic church of the Seven Daughters. Off shore are the islands of Shanvalley and Crump, with the remains of an early church, in front of the larger island of Innishturk to the north west. Close to the village are a dolmen and holy well. The top of Renvyle Hill offers a panoramic view of the surrounding countryside.

The district around Renvyle has been the location of several major films. In 1935 a screen adaption of John Millington Synge's play, *Riders to the Sea*, was filmed in Renvyle and many locals were hired as extras. In 1951 John Ford filmed the exciting beach race scenes for *The Quiet Man* at nearby Lettergesh Beach. *The Purple Taxi*, starring Peter Ustinov and Fred Astaire captured the beauty of the village and coastline. In 1989 some scenes for *The Field* with Richard Harris were filmed locally.

In 1948 Ludwig Wittgenstein, the noted philosopher, compiled his important work, *Philosophical Investigations*, in Rosroe House. Another resident of Rosroe House was Paul Henry, the artist, who painted many of the Connemara landscapes.

The area around Renvyle has much to offer those on holidays. There are many safe beaches for swimming, sailing and water skiing. Other forms of relaxation to be enjoyed include pony trekking and cycling. O'Dowd's Bar is to be recommended for a good pint and a friendly chat. The Renvyle House Hotel has a congenial atmosphere and occasionally runs murder/mystery weekends.

RECOMMENDED

Renvyle House Hotel.
Rosroe Hostel.
O'Dowd's Pub.
Renvyle Beach Caravan Park.
Renvyle Stores (Bicycle Hire).
Connemara Caravan and Camping Park.
Lettergesh Caravan Park.
Scuba Diving West.

Cleggan

Midway between Letterfrack and Clifden, at the hamlet of Moyard, follow the right hand turn for Cleggan. This will take you along the narrow coast road to Cleggan, a small fishing village on Cleggan Bay. The name Cleggan in Irish is An Cloigeann, 'the Skull', indicating a round hill above the village.

The village is somewhat rundown and untidy with fish crates and pallets strewn around the harbour area. During the summer months, there is a good deal of traffic congestion, as buses deliver and collect the passengers from Inishbofin. Oliver's Seafood Restaurant and Coyne's Bar are recommended for refreshments or a snack.

In 1601 Murrough na Maor O'Flaherty purchased land at Cleggan from the O'Halloran family. Upon his death, 25 years later, his son, Brian, inherited Cleggan Hill. In 1652 Phelim O'Neill gathered his force at Cleggan and it became one of the last mainland areas of resistance against the Parliamentary forces. The following year Cromwellian forces took control of Cleggan.

In 1804 a Martello tower was erected by the British on top of Cleggan Head as a watch tower in the event of a Napoleonic invasion. The tower stood until 1940 but now only the stump remains. In 1849 merchants in the village bought two hookers and experienced fishermen were brought from Scotland to crew them but the boats were damaged in severe weather and this plan was abandoned. In 1855 Frederick Twining, of the famous tea family, purchased 900 acres at Cleggan Bay and built Cleggan House. In an effort to relieve poverty in the district, Twining attempted to establish a fishing industry.

With so many deaths during the famine period in Connemara, several new burial grounds had to be opened. One of these was at Cleggan. In the 1860s tenants of the Law Life Assurance Company in the Cleggan area were so poor that they began sub-dividing their houses. Their landlords condemned the practice, evicted the tenants and demolished their dwellings.

In 1867 the police station was built in Cleggan. By 1872 the village of Cleggan had grown in importance with the establishment of many facilities. The piers had been extended to cater for the enlarged fishing fleet. A hotel, coastguard station, school and curling station had also been opened. The 'Leenane Head' was operating as a mail boat between Cleggan and Inishbofin, transporting passengers, supplies and mail to the island. In August 1920 a group of Volunteers burned down the RIC barracks.

In October 1927 large shoals of herring and mackerel were sighted between Cleggan and Inishbofin and the fishermen decided to set to sea. On that cold but calm night six boats left Inishbofin, four left Rossadillisk, a small townland west of Cleggan and three currachs left Bundown, a village north of Cleggan. Suddenly, when they had been to sea for two hours, a fierce storm blew up. As they attempted to row to safety, their small crafts were buffeted by the force of the waves. Many of the boats capsized with their night's catch. A long night's vigil commenced, as shawled women waited on hill tops and quaysides while boats and planes from Oranmore searched for survivors. In the tragedy which became known as 'The Cleggan Disaster', twenty-five men were lost in all, sixteen from Rossadillisk and nine from Innishbofin.

About two miles south-west of Cleggan is Omey Island, which may be reached on foot or by car at low tide. On the island are the remains of a small medieval monastery founded in the seventh century by St Feichin. West of Cleggan is Knockbrack, a chamber tomb. Near Cleggan House is the Druid's Altar, a gallery grave. On the northern shore of Cleggan Bay there is a megalithic tomb.

Richard Murphy, the poet, author of *The Last Galway Hooker*, *The Battle of Aughrim*, *The Price of Stone* and *The Cleggan Disaster*, lived in Cleggan for some years. He restored two hookers and used them in the summer months to transport passengers to Inishbofin.

A successful community project was the starting of an ice-packing plant at the harbour. Boat-building is still an active trade in the area. Cleggan is the best location for boarding boats, for the forty-five minute voyage to Inishbofin. There are several companies competing to transport passengers to and from the island. Tickets for the Dún Aengus and The Queen can by purchased in local shops. The village is a good base for many outdoor activities including pony trekking, cycling, sea angling and swimming. There is a scenic coastal route from Cleggan to Clifden via Claddaghduff but beware of the potholes.

Cleggan offers two specialists' breaks during the year. In June there is a Nature and Archaeology Weekend and in September there is a Harvest Week, based on archaeology and natural history.

RECOMMENDED

Martello Tower.
Cleggan Farm Cottages.
Coyne's Bar.
The Master's House Hostel.
Oliver's Seafood Bar.
Wild Heather Restaurant.
Harvest Festival (Sept).
Nature and Archaeology Weekend (June).
Cleggan Beach House.

Inishbofin

In the Atlantic, six miles north-west of Cleggan, lies the small quiet island of Inishbofin. The name in Irish, Inis Bó Finne means 'The Island of White Cow'. A legend exists concerning Bo Finn, the 'White Cow', which tells how two travellers landed on the island and lit a fire. An old woman nearby hit a white cow and it changed into a standing stone.

Guarim was chief of Inishbofin and he and his men protected the island. In 660 when Bishop Colman of Lindisfarne (Later St Colman) was defeated at the Synod of Whitby he left the English mission and travelled with thirty English monks and other companions to Inishbofin. Guarim gave him land to build a church. St Colman sent out tithe collectors but Guarim had several of them killed. A dispute arose between the English and Irish monks and Colman established another monastery at Balla in County Mayo. He remained abbot of both monasteries until his death in 674. There was no trace of the monastery on Inishbofin after 900.

The O'Flahertys took possession of the island in the eleventh century. Around 1380 the island was captured from the O'Flahertys by the O'Malleys to add to their sea board kingdom. Later Gráinne Ní Mhaille (Grace O'Malley, to become renowned as Granuaile), is reputed to have captured the island for her vessels. Bosco, a pirate and ally of Granuaile, built a castle at the mouth of the harbour.

In 1652 when Parliamentarians laid siege to the Aran Islands, reinforcements were despatched from Inishbofin but, following the fall of Aran, the Earl of Clanrickard reinforced the garrison on the island with Confederate troops under Colonel Cusack and Lieutenants Bourke and Costello. They were later reinforced by descendants of Bosco the Pirate. The Duke of Lorraine had offered assistance but this never arrived. Inishbofin held out until early in 1653 against Cromwellian troops and was then used as a prison camp for priests, monks, teachers and Irish soldiers. The island was designated as the Cromwellian Connacht headquarters and Cromwell's Barracks were erected at the entrance to the harbour.

Below: Cromwell's Castle

In the 1840s Lord Sligo appointed an agent, named Hildebrand, to Inishbofin but he caused so much unrest among the islanders that he was removed. In 1861 the people of the island made an appeal for help as the islanders were 'left, when sick, lying very often on a little straw, with a poor covering over them, without doctor, without medicine, to the mercy of God, to live or die.' According to the *Galway Vindicator* 28 September 1861 many of the destitute were prepared to gamble death from starvation rather than enter the workhouse.

In 1870 the Leenane Head mail boat service was inaugurated to transfer supplies and mail from Cleggan to Inishbofin. The service continued until the early 1960s. In 1892 a pier was erected on the island. There are several clocháns (beehive huts) on the island and at the south-east end is the promontory fort of Doonmore. On the western shore of the harbour is the cliff top fort of Doon Grannia. Another historical site is St. Flannan's Well. Inishshark, a smaller island to the west, can be reached by boat.

There are many safe beaches and two hotels on the island. Frequently during the winter months, the island is cut off from the mainland by rough seas. The population of about 200 is swelled considerably during the summer months as the island is a popular retreat for those seeking a peaceful holiday. Inishbofin is particularly worth visiting during the Arts Festival in May when an abundance of music, poetry and drama is featured.

RECOMMENDED

Day's Hotel.
Doonmore Hotel.
St Flannan's Well.
Cromwell's Fort.
Inishbofin Arts Festival (May).

Left: Mail boat

Above: Clifden & the Twelve Bens
Right: Waterfall at Clifden

WATERFALL AT CLIFDEN.

Clifden

Clifden is a small market town and fishing centre, fifty miles from Galway, situated against the background of the Twelve Bens. The name in Irish is 'An Clochán' (The Stepping Stones). Although unofficially regarded as the Capital of Connemara, Clifden does not have a large population.

The town is a convenient base for touring or exploring the delights of Connemara and caters for all tastes from top class hotels and gourmet restaurants to hostels and take-aways. A new one-way traffic system has helped to ease the congestion in the town centre with the heavy influx of visitors in high season. At night there is a lively atmosphere with music and 'craic' in many pubs and hotels. The dual spires of the Catholic and Protestant churches are a distinctive feature of the town.

By Irish standards, Clifden is not an old town and only two centuries ago most of the area was covered by woods, inhabited by red deer. In 1800 the D'Arcy family owned 17,000 acres around Clifden Bay. In 1812 John D'Arcy, of Kiltulla in East Galway, built a castle which became known as D'Arcy's Castle, on the Sky Road, above the town. D'Arcy also organised the building of a well-planned town and gave tenants long leases to encourage them to build houses. The town emerged rapidly with 100 slated houses, three good streets, a coastguard station, a fever hospital and an orphanage. Soon ships began anchoring in Clifden Bay and cocoa and rum were exchanged for agricultural produce. A green marble quarry opened at Letternuse and gave much employment locally.

The Church of Ireland church, built in 1820, contains a silver copy of the famous Cross of Cong, placed there in memory of the late Sir William Murphy. In 1837 the Church of Ireland Archbishop of Tuam established the Connacht Home Mission Society in Clifden. Forty children were converted to the Established Church at the Mission School leading to friction between the two denominations in the town.

In 1842 William Makepeace Thackeray visited Clifden and gave the following account: 'The first house at the entrance to Clifden is a gigantic poor-house, tall, large, ugly, comfortable; it commands the town, and looks almost as big as every one of the houses therein. The town itself is but of a few years date, and seems to thrive in its small way. Clifden Castle is a fine chateau in the neighbourhood and belongs to another owner of immense lands in Galway — Mr D'Arcy.'

The road from Galway to Clifden opened in the early 1840s and the Royal Mail and Bianconi coaches travelled this route. The Clifden Car carried mail from Dublin to Connemara.

In 1849 the D'Arcys became impoverished and the Landed Estates

Commission auctioned off the estate. From the 1820s the D'Arcys had guaranteed turf-cutting rights to the towns-people but when Thomas Eyre of Galway bought the estate he became a severe landlord and deprived them of many of their rights. Clifden did not escape the scourge of the famine and a workhouse was opened in the town. By 1849 the Clifden Poor Law had accumulated debts of £21,277 from feeding the poor and running the workhouse. Fortunately the British Association for the Relief of Distress in Ireland and Scotland was able to assist them.

Within two decades of D'Arcy establishing the town, Clifden had become such an important town that on, 17 September 1843, Daniel O'Connell addressed one of his 'monster rallies', attended by thousands of people and Young Irelanders, in the town. The attendance also included representatives of an organisation called Connemara Landlords for Repeal of the Union and an Independent Parliament for Ireland. Later the Fenians drew many volunteers from the locality.

With the construction of railways throughout Ireland the Government passed an Act of Parliament in 1872 for the construction of a line from Galway to Clifden. Although a large number of subscribers came forward, a series of complications delayed the commencement of the project. Finally in 1893 the Midland Great Western Railway line between Galway and Clifden was officially opened. Clifden had a fine station building and station master's house. The line ran alongside the road because engineers found this the most suitable route. It took twenty years to complete the stretch from Oughterard to Clifden as conditions were extremely difficult and the line had to be laid across miles of bog. Up to 1500 men were employed on the construction of the line. Some interested parties indicated that the line should have taken the coastal route through Spiddal and Roundstone to Clifden. The service from Galway to Clifden was closed on 27 April 1935 due to poor business.

Monsignor McAlpine became Parish Priest of Clifden in 1898 and served there until his death in 1932. He was a staunch supporter of the Irish Party and was to play an important role in the development of the district. Around the turn of the century the area became popular with painters and fishermen from Ireland and abroad.

In July 1905 Guglielmo Marconi, the Italian pioneer of the wireless telegraph, chose a site three miles south-west of Clifden at the bog of Derrygimlagh to erect the first Transatlantic Marconi Wireless telegraph station in Europe. Turf was used to fuel the steam-driven power plant. On 17 October 1907, the station opened and Marconi exchanged the first transatlantic radio messages with his station in Nova Scotia. Marconi also built his own narrow-gauge railway which ran for about two miles and brought supplies and equipment from the main road.

On 15 June 1919 two young men, John Alcock and Arthur Whitten Brown, flew their Vickers-Vimy two seater bi-plane from St John's, Newfoundland, Canada, non-stop across the Atlantic and crash-landed in the flat bog of Derrygimlagh, near Clifden, believing it to be a field. This was the first plane to fly across the Atlantic. The nose went down and the men scrambled out safely, close to the Marconi station. They made their way to Clifden and sent a telegram from the post office informing the world of their historic aviation achievement. A monument has been erected at the site to commemorate the historic event.

In 1914 the Fourth Battalion of the Irish Volunteers was formed in Clifden by Gerald Bartly. Following the 1918 election results, Bartly lit a celebratory bonfire for which he was jailed. He later became a Government Minister. Another young man, Thomas Whelan, was born on Sky Road, Clifden, in October 1899. He went to Dublin and joined the Volunteers. After Bloody Sunday he was arrested for the murder of a British officer and executed on 14 March 1921. In retaliation, the IRA implemented their policy of two for one (for every one of their members executed they would shoot two RIC men). On 16 March 1921 Constables Charles Reynolds and Thomas Sweeney were on patrol in Clifden when four men approached them and shot them dead. The following day reinforcements of thirty Black and Tans arrived by train from Galway to seek out Sinn Fein supporters. The Tans began drinking and looting and set fire to fourteen houses, shops and a hotel. There was fear that the entire town would catch fire. One local man was shot dead. The atrocities of the Tans encouraged many young men to join the Volunteers.

In December 1921 the inmates of Clifden workhouse were transferred by car to the County Hospital at Loughrea and the IRA took over the workhouse. Gerald Bartly received information that intelligence reports were being transmitted by British forces through the Marconi station and he ordered it destroyed. On 25 July 1922 three Republicans set fire to the station. In the Civil War, Clifden was chiefly a Republican stronghold, under the command of Michael Kilroy, who supervised the manufacture of armoured cars and bombs. In August 1922 Free State troops took over Clifden which they held until October that year when a strong force of Republicans attacked the town and set fire to the barracks. They regained control of the town and captured eighty Free State troops.

The woollen and tweed industry is one of the oldest industries in this area of Connemara. Wool was washed, dyed and left to dry against the jail walls. In the early twentieth century the Millar family took over a large converted railway building in the town and subsequently an industry emerged. Aran sweaters were also knitted locally by women in

RECOMMENDED

Barry's Hotel.
Abbeyglen Hotel.
The Blue Hostel.
Pony Trekking.
Connemara Woollen Mills.
Clifden Bay Hotel.
The Old Skillet Restaurant.
Tourist Office.
The Red Hostel.
Alcock & Brown Monument.
Alcock & Brown Hotel.
Doris's Rest.
Weaver's Workshop.
My Tea Shop.
Mannion's Pub (Traditional Music).
O'Grady's Rest.
The Derryclare Restaurant.
The Marconi Restaurant.
Cullen's Coffee Shop.
Millars.
Destry Rides Again (Rest).
Mitchell's Restaurant and Bar.
Clifden Community Arts Week.
Painting Holidays in Connemara Clifden Glen.
The Celtic Shop.
The Green Shop and Gallery.
Dan O'Hara's Homestead.
Connemara Heritage Tours.
Rockglen Hotel.

the cottages. The market gained momentum and Millars tweed sold exceptionally well, especially to American visitors. Millars Tweeds was the only industry in Clifden until the 1970s. Today it is still a thriving business and their shop stocks shawls, tweeds and Aran sweaters from the Gaeltacht home industries. There are a number of other good quality craft shops and art galleries in the town.

One of the highlights of the social calendar in Clifden is the Connemara Pony Show, held annually in mid-August. The show features equestrian events along with displays by the small, shaggy Connemara ponies. The one day event creates a festive spirit with street traders, bands, exhibitions and competitions of home knitting and cooking. Gaelic speakers blend easily with Europeans and Americans. Along with the Pony Show there are two other lively events held each September, the Country Blues Festival and the Clifden Community Arts Week.

For those seeking more leisurely pursuits there are many pleasant walks, drives and cycles in the vicinity. A short walk below the town, the Owenglen River gushes over boulders to create the spectacular Owenglen cascade. In season the salmon can be seen leaping as they make their way upstream. There are many good beaches in the locality. The Sky Road, to the west of the town, runs alongside the indented coastline, giving breathtaking views of the sea, islands and mountains. For many years the film actor, Peter O'Toole, had a cottage on Sky Road.

A new addition to the amenities of the area is Clifden Glen, a self-catering complex. Four miles from Clifden is Dan O'Hara's Homestead, a pre-1840 farm with its modern reconstruction of an ancient lake dwelling (a crannóg) and tearooms which are open to visitors and school tours between April – September. Recently a neolithic court tomb, 5500 years old, was discovered by archaeologists, close to the Sky Road.

CLIFDEN - ALCOCK & BROWN MEMORIAL

Ballyconneely

Ballyconneely is a small hamlet, six miles south of Clifden on the Clifden to Roundstone Road. The village, reached by a winding road above a rocky coastline, is situated on the isthmus between Ballyconneely Bay and Mannin Bay. The name Ballyconneely in Irish is, Baile Conaola (Conaola's Townland). Mannin Bay consists of several beaches including the Coral Strand, a glittering beach composed of minute corallines and white sand. Boats and tackle for blue shark and deep sea fishing can be hired in the village.

Within the vicinity of the village you will find much of historical interest. There is the small church of St Flannan of Bunowen. Donal O'Flaherty and his wife Granuaile built a castle here which became their main stronghold and where they brought up their three children. In the mid-eighteenth century Richard Geoghegan, a descendant of a Cromwellian transplantee, chose a site by the coast to build a castle from the stones of the O'Flaherty castle. In 1780 Geoghegan built a folly on Doon Hill. Geoghegan also succeeded in reclaiming large tracts of land from the sea.

Between 1939-45 there was a watch-tower in operation on Doon Hill. In recent times archaeologists discovered a small village of six fortified houses which date back to the Iron Age, circa 500 BC, at Óilean na Lochlannaigh (the Island of the Vikings) near Ballyconneely.

Westwards, close to the Bunowen Quay road, at Aillebrack, is the well of the Seven Daughters. The nearby beach is protected by extensive sand-dunes. Closeby is the 18-hole Ballyconneely Championship Golf Course, also known as the Connemara Golf Course, which was established in 1973.

There are several interesting islands off the coast. In 1836 a lighthouse was erected on Slyne Head. On nearby Chapel Island are the remains of St Cáilin's chapel, dating from the twelfth century. St Cáilin is the patron saint of fishermen and there is an annual pilgrimage on 13 November to his holy well at Keeraunmore. At Dunloughan Beach there are prehistoric dwellings dating from 2000 BC.

Barr an Bhaile Barn is noted for its pancakes and crêpes and its wide selection of Connemara photographs. Keogh's Pub is a favourite gathering place.

RECOMMENDED

Connemara Golf Course.
Erriseask House Hotel.
Ballyconneely Pony Show (July).
Castle remains.
Ballyconneely Information & Community Development Office.
Sea fishing.
Barr an Bhaile Barn.
Slyne Head.
Connemara Smokehouse.
Coral Beach.
Mannin Strand.
Keogh's Pub.

Roundstone

Roundstone is a small coastal fishing village, about nine miles east of Ballyconneely. The village is well sheltered by the Errisbeg Mountain, rising to 987 feet. The attractive harbour faces across to the low lying islands in Bertraghboy Bay. The name Roundstone is an English corruption of Cloch na Rón, the Stone of the Seals.

The village is a photographer's delight where a full roll of film could be run off within a two mile radius. Roundstone Bog, dotted with a hundred tiny lakes, is a favourite haunt of botanists, from home and abroad, who come to study the rare plants and heathers. For those self-catering, they can buy fresh fish directly from the fishermen on the pier. Lobsters are a speciality. The village offers a variety of restaurants and pubs for the weary traveller to choose from.

In the early nineteenth century Alexander Nimmo, a Scottish engineer, built the village and harbour and its first settlers were Scottish fishermen. In 1820 a shoal of whales were stranded on the beach at Roundstone and the locals cut them up for food.

Within a decade, from the early 1830s, several denominations built churches in the village. In 1832 the Catholic church was built and three years later the Franciscans opened a monastery. In the early 1840s a Church of Ireland and a Presbyterian church were opened. The Bible Society also established a small haven for fishermen in the village. By the 1840s there were 75 houses in the village with many of the men employed in the fishing industry.

In 1842 William Makepeace Thackeray visited Roundstone courthouse, and gave the following account: 'The next day the Petty Sessions were held at Roundstone, a little town which has lately sprung up near the noble bay of that name. I was glad to see some specimens of Connemara litigation, as also to behold at least 1000 beautiful views that lie on the five miles road between the town and Ballyconneely all in rivers and rocks, mountains and seas, green plains and bright skies. How (for the 150th time) can pen and ink set you down? There is little to see in the town of Roundstone, except a Presbyterian chapel in process of erection that seems big enough to accommodate the Presbyterians of the country; and a sort of lay convent, being a community of brothers of the Third Order of St. Francis.'

Two miles west of Roundstone on the Ballyconneely Road, are two of the main attractions of the area, Dog's Bay and Gorteen Bay. They are formed in the long curving shore of a sand spit which connects a mile long granite island to the mainland. In the 1890s Robert Praeger, the distinguished botanist, conducted a major survey into the flora and fauna in the district.

In September 1920 during the War of Independence, the Third Battalion of the Irish Volunteers organised in Roundstone under Jim King. In April 1922 a Pro-Treaty meeting was held in the village and a British destroyer had to evacuate the coastguard station. With the outbreak of the Civil War in June 1922, phone lines were cut in the locality. When a fever epidemic gripped the district the local dispensary doctor complained that he was unable to carry out his duties due to the breakdown in communications.

In the 1960s the writer Kate O'Brien moved to live in the area and bought a house which was known locally as the 'Fort'. The building had previously been a dispensary. Kate O'Brien whose novels include *Without My Cloak, The Last of Summer* and *The Ante-Room* said of the area; 'Roundstone resembles a quaint fishing village in Normandy or Brittany.' Later the pop singer, Sting, bought the house and lived there for a number of years.

The beauty of the area did not go unnoticed by the film makers and in 1973 director John Huston, shot scenes on the pier for his thriller *The Mackintosh Man*, starring Paul Newman and James Mason. In 1991 Dog's Bay was chosen as a location for *Into the West* with Gabriel Byrne and Ellen Barkin. This exciting tale of two young itinerant boys travelling west with their white horse was widely praised. Roundstone also featured in the film *Hear My Song*, which starred Ned Beatty and Adrian Dunbar and centred around an adventure in the life of the singer, Josef Locke.

In 1983 the Industrial Development Authority (IDA) established a number of small scale industries in the old Franciscan Monastery, with the erection of a number of craft workshops. Among the small industries at the centre are the manufacture of musical instruments, a pottery, a silversmith and a coffee shop. During the summer months the Heritage Museum in Roundstone Hall is open to the public.

RECOMMENDED

IDA Craft Centre.
Connolly's Bar.
Malachy Kearn's Craft Shop.
Hilltop Bar.
Roundstone House Hotel.
Roundstone Hall Heritage Museum.
Bicycle Hire.
Pony Trekking.
Beola Restaurant.
Gurteen Beach Caravan Park.
Salmon & Lobster Festival in June.
Regatta in July.
O'Dowd's Bar and Restaurant.
Eldon's Hotel.

Ballynahinch

From Roundstone take the curving coast road in a northward direction. At the second junction it would be advisable to take a detour at a signpost indicating Ballynahinch. A short distance along this road, concealed in the woods, is Ballynahinch Castle (the present castle dates from the eighteenth century). It takes its name Baile na hInse, (Townland of the Island), from a small castle crowned island (crannóg) in Ballynahinch Lake, situated at the foot of the 1900 foot Benletttery, one of the Twelve Bens. The district has magnificent views of this mountain range which dominate the landscape.

Originally the area around Ballynahinch belonged to the O'Keelys and it later came into the possession of Donal O'Flaherty, husband of Gráinne Ní Mhaille (Granuaile), who built the small castle in the lake. The stones are reputed to have been taken from Toombeola Abbey. Donal O'Flaherty's son, Murrough, defended the castle against invaders from the east. The O'Flahertys built two religious houses in the district; in 1356 the Carmelite Friary in Ballynahinch and in 1427 the Dominican Friary at Toombeola.

After the Cromwellian victory in 1651 most of Connemara was taken from the O'Flahertys and granted to the Martins. The Martin estate was the most extensive in Connemara, covering 200,000 acres. In 1792 Richard Martin, one of the most famous members of the family inherited the estate. He was a duellist and lover of animals, once known as 'Hairtrigger Dick' but nicknamed 'Humanity Dick' by King George IV because he was a founder member of the Royal Society for the Prevention of Cruelty to Animals. He became a member of Parliament and a magistrate for Connemara and was noted for his lenient sentences.

Following the famine of 1847 the bulk of the Martin estate, consisting of mountains and bog, was mortgaged to the Law Assurance Company of London.

With the introduction of the Galway to Clifden line in 1895 Ballynahinch saw an influx of more tourists to the area. In 1926 the property was bought by Prince Ranjit Sinjhi, the Indian cricketer, who retained it until his death in 1933. In 1945 the building became a hotel known as the Ballynahinch Castle Hotel. The hotel, ideally situated above the Owenmore River, is still a thriving business today.

RECOMMENDED

Ballynahinch Castle Hotel.
Owenmore River.
Old Castle on island.
Ballynahinch Fishery.

South Galway

Most travellers approaching Galway city from the Dublin Road turn right at Oranmore, thereby missing the attractions of south Galway. The area encompasses rich pasture land, unspoilt villages and many keep castles and towers. A stop should be made at Clarinbridge and Kilcolgan with their award-winning restaurants and thriving oyster industry. The village of Kinvara, bordering on the Burren, with its medieval banquets in Dunguaire Castle, should not be missed. From Kinvara branch inland to Gort, which is the Heritage town for County Galway. The area is noted for its associations with the Irish Literary Revival movement with Edward Martyn at Tullira Castle, Lady Gregory at Coole House and W B Yeats at Thoor Ballylee. The latter two centres are open to the public but unfortunately Coole House has been demolished and has been replaced by a visitors' centre. Travellers can walk the grounds of the demesne and inspect the famous autograph tree. Thoor Ballylee has been restored by Ireland West Tourism and has an audio-visual presentation, bookshop and tearooms.

From Gort branch eastwards to Woodford and then northwards along the towns and villages close to the course of the River Shannon. Portumna, ideally situated on the river has much to offer from a marina to the historic Portumna Castle and Friary. Farther north is the hamlet of Clonfert which was once a place of learning. From Clonfert return westwards, following the signposts for Loughrea which sits snugly on the shores of Lough Rea. The town is worth exploring to visit the cathedral and other historical landmarks in the district. The circuit is then completed by returning to the main Dublin to Galway Road at the sleepy village of Craughwell.

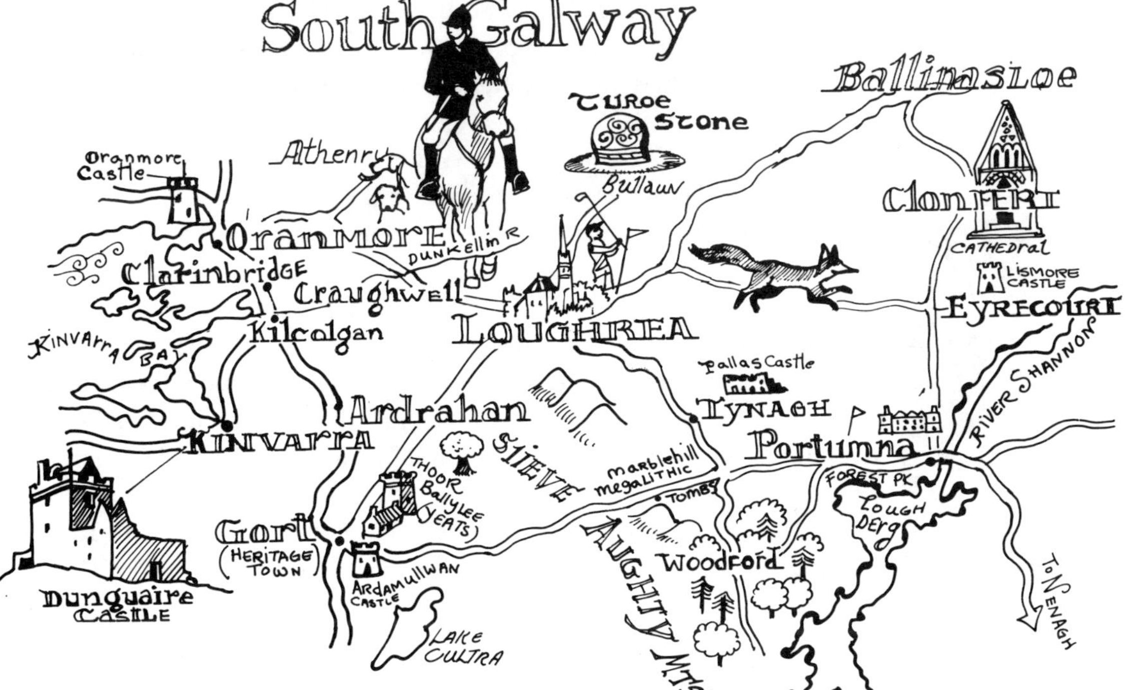

Oranmore

In Oranmore in the County Galway
One pleasant evening in the month of May,
I spied a damsel
She was young and handsome,
Her beauty fairly took my breath away.

This is the opening verse of the popular song *The Galway Shawl.*

Oranmore is a small, tidy village at the junction of the Dublin to Galway Road and the Limerick to Galway Road and about five miles east of Galway. A new bye-pass diverts heavy traffic from the south and east around the village, returning it to some of its former tranquillity. The Irish name of the village, situated at the head of Galway Bay, is Uarán Mor or Órán Mór (Big Well or Big Cold Spring).

In 1487 Oranmore was granted a wardenship by William Joyce. In the sixteenth century the Earl of Clanrickard built a castle on the shore of the bay, commanding the main road from Dublin. According to the *Annals of the Four Masters* in 1597, following the capture of Athenry Castle, Red Hugh O'Donnell, Earl of Tyrconnell, stayed overnight at the castle. In 1641 intelligence reports informed the Earl of Clanrickard that a large force from Connacht was marching on Galway Castle. When the locals rebelled and joined the confederates, he placed a strong garrison in Oranmore Castle and dispatched 140 carriages of wheat, malt and supplies to the castle and from there they were transported by sea to Galway. He then mustered 700 foot and 200 horse soldiers but discovered that the only two land routes to the castle were blocked to the enemy. He proceeded to cut off their supplies and placed strong garrisons on his castles at Oranmore, Claregalway and Tirellan. In 1643 Captain Willoughly, Governor of Galway, surrendered the castles and the land was fortified but in a patent of 1662 much of the property, including Oranmore, was returned to the sixth Earl of Clanrickard. Four years later he granted Oranmore to Walter Athy and his descendants, the Blakes, held much of the area for several centuries.

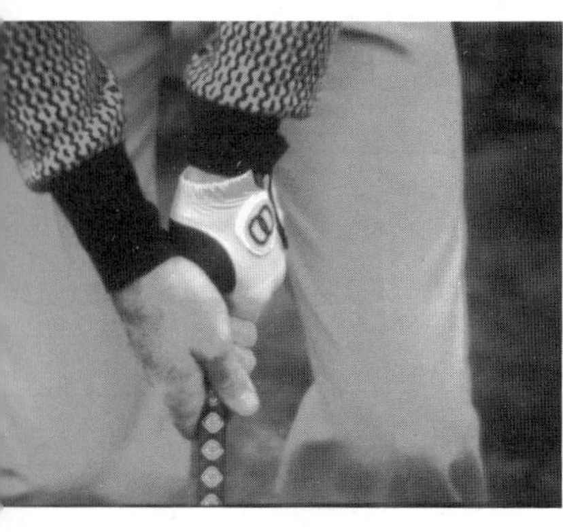

Oranmore Castle remained a ruin for many years until the writer, Anita Leslie, occupied and restored it to its former glory. Anita Leslie was born in 1914 and became a prolific writer, producing her war memoirs and several biographies including *Train to Nowhere, Love in a Nutshell, Jennie* and *Mr Frewen of England*. Besides Oranmore Castle there were several more castles in the district including Moneyduff Castle, Renville Castle (of the Lynch-Athy family), Ardfry Castle and Creganna Castle.

In 1780 the Church of Ireland church was built in the village. In 1803 the Roman Catholic church was erected but on 6 January 1839 on 'The

Night of the Big Wind', the complete roof of the church was blown away. Early in the nineteenth century a pier was constructed beside the castle in which boats from Connemara could land their supplies of turf. It was not unknown for poteen to be included in the cargo. In May 1836 Dominick Browne, an MP for Mayo was created an Irish Peer, with the title 'Baron Oranmore.'

In 1842 William Makepeace Thackeray, gave the following account of the village: 'Oranmore, with an old castle in the midst of the village, woods, and park-plantations abound about, and the bay beyond it, has a pretty and romantic look; and the drive, of four miles thence to Galway, is the most picturesque part, perhaps, of the fifty miles ride from Limerick. The road is tolerably wooded.'

On 1 August 1851 the Midland Great Western Railway Company opened Oranmore railway station with the arrival of the first train on the Dublin to Oranmore line. The Dublin to Mullingar section of the line was completed in 1848 and extended to Oranmore in 1851. Oranmore station was used to transport livestock, fish and turf to Galway and Dublin. The line was also used to transfer prisoners from Galway Jail to England.

In 1886 the Presentation Sisters built a convent in Oranmore which was opened three years later and hundreds of children walked from the surrounding districts to attend the school. From 1947 the convent took in boarders.

In 1914 a company of Irish Volunteers was formed in Oranmore and they drilled locally. In Easter Week 1916 they attacked the local RIC barracks but failed to capture it. Within ten days of the rising, practically all the Oranmore Volunteers were detained in Galway Jail. There is a statue to Liam Mellowes, a leader of the 1916 rising, in the centre of the village.

On 21 August 1920, following the ambush of five RIC men and the killing of one of them, police and British troops burned several houses and premises in the village. In December 1920 Black and Tans ambushed a cart with four men, killing one of them, Joe Athy. Commander Lewis D'Arcy was captured at Oranmore station and after being tortured, he was shot dead by a Black and Tan.

There are many ringforts and souterrains worth visiting in the area. One of the best known features of the village is Mac Donagh's Pub with its traditional thatched roof. From Oranmore on a clear day it is possible to see the Hills of Clare and even the Aran Islands. A recent amenity to the area is the Galway Bay Golf and Country Club which contains a championship golf course and leisure centre at Renville Park. Close by there is a picnic area and park.

RECOMMENDED

Oranmore Castle.
Oranmore Lodge Hotel.
Keane's County Venue.
The Shawl Festival (July).
Church of the Immaculate Conception.
Mac Donagh's Pub.
The Green Briar Inn.
Galway Bay Golf and Country Club.
Rinville Woodland Park (free).

Clarinbridge

The village of Clarinbridge is south of Oranmore, on the Galway to Gort Road, close to the head of Dunbulcaun Bay, the most easterly inlet of Galway Bay. The name Clarinbridge derives from the bridge across the Clarin River and the river took its name from the plank bridge that succeeded the original hurdle crossing. According to P W Joyce, the name translates into Irish as Droichead an Chláirín, (the Bridge of the Little Plain). Other sources refer to the village as Ath-Cliath Meadh-Raighe (the Hurdle Bridge of the Old District).

Beside the Clarinbridge River there is an earthwork which is reputed to have been a medieval fortification. On the east coast close to the Ballynamanagh bridge, is Dunbulcaun, a ringfort with a motte-type, central mound. Two miles west at Rathgurreen there is another ringfort.

In 1837 Samuel Lewis wrote: 'A patent was granted in 1820 for a market to be held in Clarinbridge on Tuesday, principally for oats and wheat. Fairs for pigs and horses were held in February, May, August and October. There were 450 inhabitants in the village.'

Adjoining the village is the demesne of Kilcornan House in which T N Redington, landlord of the village resided. The house incorporating the tower of a fifteenth century castle was the original residence of Norah Burke, a cruel chieftainess of the Clanrickard family. The house is now a home for mentally handicapped people. Today there are magnificent grounds laid out with picnic tables. In the thirteenth century a small church was erected in the grounds, which is still in a good state of repair.

In Easter week 1916 Volunteers from the surrounding towns and villages in the county marched to Clarinbridge where they were met by Liam Mellowes and the Clarinbridge Volunteers.

In 1954 an Oyster Festival was initiated in Clarinbridge due to the local community's deep involvement in the oyster industry, with extensive rich oyster beds in the vicinity. This festival has flourished and attracts an international clientele for the annual celebrations each September. Most of the activities takes place in a marquee, around Paddy Burke's Oyster Tavern, the famous oyster pub. The traveller should also check out the beautiful displays of ornamental glass in Clarinbridge Crystal. Those in search of knitwear or crafts should visit Abbey Handcrafts and the Woollen Forge. Traugh Beach, three miles from Kinvarra is suitable for swimming. Kilcornaun Wood Forest trail commences close to the Clarin River.

On facing page: Oyster festival

RECOMMENDED

Clarinbridge Crystal and Coffee Shop.

Abbey Handcrafts.

St Joseph's, Kilcornan Centre.

St Cornan's Church.

Woollen Forge.

Paddy Burke's Oyster Tavern.

The Annunciation of the Blessed Virgin Mary Catholic Church.

Clarinbridge Oyster Festival (Sept).

Traugh Beach.

Kilcolgan

RECOMMENDED

Moran's of the Weir Oyster Pub.
Drumacoo Church.
Dunkellin River.
Kilcolgan Flea Market (Sunday).
Power's Woollen Mills.
Raftery's Restaurant.

Two miles south of Clarinbridge, on the Galway to Gort Road, is the small village of Kilcolgan. The name in Irish, Cill Cholgáin (Colga's Church) evolves from Colga, a disciple of Adamnan, a sixth century saint. In 580 St Colga left Iona to establish a monastery here. A Church of Ireland church was later built on the site and only the ruins of the church remain today.

The following reference to Kilcolgan appears in the *Annals of the Four Masters*: 'AD 1600, O'Connell and his forces proceeded on their march through the hills of the Burren, without receiving a battle until they arrived on the hill of Cnoc an Ghearráin, between Kilcolgan and Galway.'

Kilcolgan Castle, situated at the mouth of the Dunkellin River, and Tyrone House, built in 1770, were owned by the St George family. Two miles south-east of Kilcolgan, at Kilbieran, there was an early monastic settlement, with an early church inside a large enclosure. In 1830 the north wing was added to the building. Close to Kilcolgan a narrow road leads to the ancient monastic site of Drumacoo, dedicated to the sixth century Sister Sourney. The south doorway is decorated in early gothic style, circa 1200. In the thirteenth century Abbot O'Halgaith allowed foreign scholars, the sick and the poor to stay at the friary. Outside the friary wall there is a holy well.

Each September the Galway Oyster 'Pearl' of the Year presents the first oyster to the first citizen of the city, the Mayor of Galway, at the opening of the Galway International Oyster Festival. The famous Moran's of the Weir Oyster Pub and Restaurant is situated at the mouth of the Dunkellin River.

Drumacoo doorway

Ardrahan

Ardrahan is a quiet village, seventeen miles from Galway on the Galway to Limerick Road. The name in Irish is Ard Rathain (Height of the Fort or Raithin, Height of the Ferns). The main features of the village are the thatched roofs of Jimmy Burke's pub and a cottage and an old water pump in the centre of the market square. Many of the houses are freshly whitewashed. A mile east of the village there exists a rich heritage of ancient remains with a pillarstone, a ringfort and several souterrains.

In the ninth century Ardrahan was the stronghold of the O'Heynes, Lords of Aidhne. In 1225 they defeated a strong force of Anglo-Normans. Their victory is recalled in the song, *The West's Awake*. In 1236 Richard de Burgo conquered Galway and awarded Ardrahan to Maurice Fitzgerald who built a square keep castle in the village and made it one of his strongholds. The remains of this stone castle are still standing.

The Church of Ireland church was erected on the site of an ancient church. In the adjoining graveyard there is the stump of a round tower. In 1605 a patent was granted for a Monday market to be held in the village. Close to the village, Lord Clanmorris built Cregaclare, a large house which incorporates a mausoleum, as the family seat. A mile north-east of the village is the eighteenth century Castle Taylor. On the road from Ardrahan to Loughrea, the Burkes, the local landlords, built another tower house, known as Creagh Castle, in the late fifteenth century. At the turn of the century Creagh housed a still for poteen.

The tower-house of Tullira, near Ardrahan, in the barony of Kiltartan, was built in the sixteenth century by the Clanrickard Burkes, in the centre of their demesne. In 1598, the Catholic Martin (or Martyn) family, bought the building. In 1873 Edward Martyn inherited the estate, when he was only fourteen. He went on to become a poet, playwright and patron of the arts and did much to encourage Lady Gregory and W B Yeats in the foundation of the National Theatre. In 1882 Yeats strongly objected when Martyn commissioned the architect, George Ashlin, to add on a Tudor extension to Tullira. Following Martyn's death, without an heir, the property passed to the Hemphill family.

By the early 1800s Ardrahan had become an enterprising village. Flannel spun locally was sold at the Oranmore market. The village had a dispensary, a police barracks, and Petty Sessions were held every fortnight. Around 1800 the Catholic church was built. The building was so badly constructed that it soon required a new roof. There was a national school and a number of pay schools. The area had a number of mineral springs and iron ore was mined locally.

RECOMMENDED

Water Pump in Square.
St Teresa's Catholic Church.
Jimmy Burke's Thatch Pub.
Quinn Loughnane Memorial Hall.
Ardrahan Inn.
Creagh Castle.
Tullira House.

Kinvara

At Kilcolgan, leave the main road to Gort and take a right hand turn to Kinvara (or Kinvarra). Kinvarra is a small, picturesque fishing village at the south-east corner of Galway Bay. Its position at the edge of the limestone landscape of the Burren and at the head of the bay accounts for its name in Irish, Cinn Mhara (Sea Headlands or The Head of the Sea). Near the seashore there are two extensive caverns.

The village always has an appealing atmosphere with its restaurants and brightly painted shops and houses with their window boxes. The harbour, festooned with fishing boats and lobster pots, has served as a backdrop in many photographs and postcards. The village is the ideal location for exploring the Burren and southwards into County Clare.

In the fifteenth century Rory More O'Shaughnessy captured the Castle of Doon from Flan Killikelly, demolished it and built a new one in its place, called Doongorey or Dunguaire Castle, on a jutted promontory beside the bay. In 1642 it became the property of Thomas Taylor who built a wall encircling the castle. For a period the building became the residence of the Martyns of Tullira. The original, Dún Ghuaire, was the seat of the sixth century King Guaire Aidhneach of Connacht. The castle featured in the legend of the King's Easter Dishes. In 1924 the castle was bought and refurbished by Oliver St John Gogarty, the noted literary figure and surgeon. In 1954 the castle was acquired by Christobel Lady Ampthill who finished the refurbishing. From 1966 the castle was opened to the public and commenced medieval banquets. Six years later Dunguaire Castle was purchased by Shannon Free Airport Development Company. Nearby there is a ringfort, strewn with boulders. Also close to the castle is Tobermacduagh Holy Well.

In 1773 J French built a pier and by 1808 it had been converted into an ambitious dock, accommodating 150 tons. Seaweed, which was a valuable commodity for farming was landed here in vast quantities. A steam ship ran a regular service to Galway from the dock. By the mid-nineteenth century Kinvarra was a significant village with exports of grain and agricultural produce. During the famine of 1845, conditions were so bad around Kinvarra that Robert Gregory, who had large holdings around the village, donated £25 towards distress and became Chairman of the Kinvarra Relief Committee.

Five miles west of Kinvarra is Doorus House where Baron de Basterot, a writer and traveller, once lived. He donated land for a Catholic church to be erected in the village. He entertained many celebrities at his home. In 1898 Lady Gregory, W B Yeats and Edward Martyn met at Doorus House to mark the establishment of the Irish Literary Theatre movement, out of which the Abbey Theatre Company grew in 1904. Later Doorus House became a youth hostel. In 1854 Francis A Fahy, the composer of ballads was born in Kinvarra. One of his most popular ballads was *The Queen of Connemara*.

In 1979 film director, Andrew V McLaglen, chose Dunguaire Castle and the surrounding countryside to shoot scenes for the film, *Northsea Hijack*, with Roger Moore and James Mason. The castle featured as the home of Moore, who is assigned to apprehend a gang who hijack a North Sea oil rig.

Kinvarra has a strong tradition of trading by sea with communities along the Connemara coast. This legacy is celebrated every August in the village with Cruinniú na mBád (Gathering of the Boats). In the weekend activities, a wide range of boats, including dark sailed Galway hookers, with cargoes of turf, sail across the bay.

RECOMMENDED

Dunguaire Castle Banquets.
Partners Restaurant.
Féile na mBád (August).
Doorus House Hostel.
Winkles Hotel (Music).
Village Crafts.
Sayres Restaurant.
Johnson's Hostel.

Below: Doonagore Castle, County Clare, view to the Aran Islands

Gort

Gort is a medium sized market town on the Galway to Ennis Road, situated in a gap between the Slieve Aughty Mountains and the Burren to the south. The name in Irish is An Gort, (The Field) or Gort Inse Guaire, (Field of Guaire's Island). The town takes its name from King Guaire, the sixth century King of Connacht, who built a castle here. He had a reputation for his generosity and it was said that his right arm, his giving arm, was longer than his left. One legend recalls how Guaire was sitting down to dinner when mysteriously the plates disappeared out the windows. He quickly followed them on horseback and soon met St Colman who had just finished a seven year fast and had eaten the food. The king was impressed by his ingenuity and granted him lands at Kilmacduagh where he built a monastery, one of the oldest in Europe.

Above: W B Yeats 1865 - 1939

Below: The Autograph tree, Coole Park

The area around the town is notable for its landscape of grey stone walls and stone-strewn fields. The eighteenth century weigh-house in the town square has recently been restored. There is a strong tradition of Irish music in the locality and many pubs stage sessions at night.

Five miles south of Gort is Ardamullwan Castle, where in the Middle Ages the O'Shaughnessy family had their main stronghold on the site of the old military barracks. In 1567 the castle was claimed by Dermot O'Shaughnessy, on the death of his borther, Roger. A long dispute followed between Dermot and his nephew John, which resulted in both of them being killed. Five miles south-west of Gort is Fiddaun Castle, another of the O'Shaughnessy strongholds in Connacht. In the seventeenth century the confiscated O'Shaughnessy lands were granted to the Verekers family (later Viscount Gort).

In the middle of the eighteenth century Gort was a poor town of little importance but, under the direction of Lord Gort it developed rapidly and by the beginning of the next century it had become a prosperous commercial centre. Broad, well-planned streets were laid out and tall houses and business premises were erected. There was an air of prosperity as wealth and employment increased with the opening of new small industries. A large flour mill was constructed, producing 7000 barrels annually, which serviced farmers and merchants in the surrounding countryside. The opening of a brewery and tannery yard gave additional employment. Soon Gort had become established as a market town, holding a market every Saturday. Sheep and cattle fairs were held in May, August and November and a large pig fair on St Patrick's Day.

In 1815 a courthouse was opened and the Quarter Sessions for County Galway were held there each October. Petty Sessions were held every Saturday. There was also a revenue officer, a constabulary station and the O'Shaughnessy Castle which was later demolished and replaced by a cavalry barracks with billets for eight officers and eighty eight men and stables for 160 horses. The Dublin to Galway and Galway to Limerick mail coaches ran through the town.

In June 1825 the local doctor, Dr French asked the people of Gort to start collecting for a new church which resulted in acquiring the sum of £250. He intended turning the old church into a school and hoped the local gentry would donate a site for a new church. Lord Gort asked the bishop to pick whatever site he liked on his property. The rent was fixed at a pepper corn per annum, for the lease forever. The Catholic church was built that same year. Four years later Lord Gort donated a site to the Church of Ireland.

In the nineteenth century Robert Gregory employed two English bailiffs to oversee work on his 600 acres of Coole estate. One supervised walling his demesne, a limestone quarry on the estate providing stones for the walls. Gregory built a large, three storey rectangular house overlooking Coole Lake, with a view of the Burren in the background. His small tenants lived in cabins and the cottiers in mud cabins. By 1837 there were 600 houses and 3500 people living in Gort and its environs.

In 1842 William Makepeace Thackeray visited Gort and gave the following uncomplimentary opinion: 'Then we passed the plantation of Lord Gort's Castle of Loughcoole, and presently came to the town which bears his name, or vice versa. It is a regularly built little place, with a square and street, but it looked as if it wondered how the deuce it got into the midst of such a desolate country, and seemed to bore itself considerably. It had nothing to do, and no society.'

William Gregory served for many years as Chairman of the Gort Board of Guardians and was appointed High Sheriff in 1851. With the advent of the railway he appealed to his fellow landowners not to hold out for too high a price for land required by the railway company. The Mullingar to Galway extension opened to the public on 1 August 1851. With the famine of 1861 Gregory cut trees on Coole demesne and distributed them as fuel to the poor of the locality. The Gregorys made generous contributions to the Gort Relief Fund.

On 3 March 1880 Sir William Gregory married Isabella Augusta Persse. She was the twelfth of sixteen children and the youngest and smallest of seven daughters of Dudley Persse. Lady Gregory invited inmates of Gort workhouse to Coole for a day and would also bring gifts to the institution. In 1881 with land agitation in the area, a local man was boycotted for giving lodgings to a police officer. The following year the tenants of Sir William Gregory refused to pay their rent, forcing him to implement 'extreme measures'. The police advised him to leave for his own safety and on returning the following summer there was relative peace due to the intervention of Fr Jerome Fahy, a young curate in Gort. Gregory then reached an amicable settlement with his tenants over rents.

Lady Gregory was to play an active part in the Irish Literary Revival at the turn of the century. Her home at Coole Park became the retreat of most of the leading writers of the day including Sean O'Casey, Augustus John, John Millington Synge and W B Yeats who convalesced here when he was ill. In the grounds there is a copper beech tree on which her guests carved their initials. They included Sean O'Casey, Synge, AE (George Russell), GBS (George Bernard Shaw) and Jack Yeats. When Lady Gregory died in 1932, aged eighty, the house and estate passed to the state. The house was demolished in 1941.

In 1917 W B Yeats bought a nearby sixteenth century tower called Thoor Ballylee for £35. He renovated the building and lived in it until 1929. The tower became immortalised in his poems and he wrote *The Tower* volume of poems. A plaque commemorates his spell there:

'I, the poet William Yeats
With old mill boards and sea-green slates
And smithy work from the Gort forge,
Restored this tower for my wife George;
And may these characters remain
When all in ruin once again.'

Bord Fáilte took over responsibility for the tower and transformed it into a museum which is now open to the public. Near Thoor Ballylee was the home of Mary Hynes, the miller's daughter, with whom the blind fiddler, Antoine Raftery, was in love and dedicated a song.

In 1968 the area between Gort and Loughrea was chosen as the principal location for a major film, *Alfred the Great*, starring David Hemmings and Michael York. A complete Saxon village was built by the film-makers. Many young local men grew beards and wore their hair long to be hired as extras for the battle scenes.

Close to the town is the subterranean River Beagh which flows through a ravine called the Hadle and circular basins called the Church, the Punch-bowl and Beggar Man's Hole. In the twelfth century the castle of Kiltartan was erected nearby. The amphitheatre formed by the crater is now a picnic area. Recently some interests in the town have sought to have the name An Gort, replaced by the more meaningful, Gort Inse Guaire. Gort has been selected as the Heritage Town for County Galway.

RECOMMENDED

Coole Demesne.
Glynn's Hotel.
Weigh House.
Thoor Ballylee.
Sullivan's Royal Hotel.
O'Gradys, Spring Nite Club.
Luke Kelly's Pub (Music).
St Colman's Catholic Church.
Ardamullivan Castle.

Woodford

The Barracks

From Gort follow the road eastwards through the Slieve Aughty Mountains. At a crossroads follow the signpost due south to the village of Woodford. The attractive village is situated among picturesque woods, at the south-eastern corner of County Galway. The Irish name for Woodford is An Ghraig or Graig na Muilte Iarainn (The Village of the Iron Works), indicating the ironworks which once flourished in the locality. About one and a half miles north of the village there is a ring of seven standing stones, giving some indication of its ancient history. In the twelfth century some of the De Burgo family settled in Woodford, which was then known as Upper Ballinakill.

Woodford is the headquarters for the East Galway Family History Society, based in the Heritage Centre. At the centre people can trace their roots and take guided tours of the local prehistoric tombs and stone circles. On a fine day it is worth climbing Ben Hill for the panoramic view overlooking an extensively wooded landscape, which extends to the River Shannon with a backdrop of the Tipperary Mountains.

The majority of sources agree that the village came into existence in the latter part of the seventeenth century because in 1690 John Stevens, an officer in King James's army, referred to an iron mills operating there. The Crossdale family who ran the operation, built houses for their employees. An abundance of oak forests were cut down to supply charcoal, which was one of the main ingredients in the production of iron. The Woodford River ran through the village and powered a cornmill which gave additional employment. Medium sized boats could navigate the river up to Perch Hole, below Geeran's Bridge. Other ore was transported to the mill from Lough Derg. Following the Battle of Aughrim in July 1691 Baron de Ginkell pursued Patrick Sarsfield as far as Woodford. While passing Piper's Pier, Sarsfield hid guns in the wood and, in an effort to confuse the enemy, he ordered that his horse's shoes should be reversed.

Before the opening of the ironworks, the tanning of leather was carried on in the district. The tannery was later converted into a graveyard. In 1780 the Crossdales sold their Woodford properties in order to raise finance to form a company of Grattan's Volunteers. In 1814 troops of the 28th Regiment from headquarters took over a temporary barracks under Captain Frank Kennedy. They set about tracking down the rebels, known as 'The Ribbonmen', who were originally the Catholic defenders in the northern counties of Ireland. Two of their leaders, Gibbons and Garland, were arrested and hanged. Without their leaders the Ribbonmen sought refuge in the mountains.

For a period, salt was manufactured in Woodford, following the closure of the ironworks. Thomas Burke, of Marble Hall, used the cinders from the works to build roads in his estate. The Keary family ran another small industry which manufactured nails. Antoine Raftery (1784-1835), the blind poet, often visited his friend, John Sweeney, a weaver, in Woodford.

During the Land War of the 1880s, Woodford gained national fame as there was strong resistance locally to the notorious Marquess of Clanrickard, an absentee landlord. One Woodford eviction in particular is long remembered. On 20 August 1886 a courageous group of Woodford men gathered to defend the home of Thomas Saunders. Saunders and his family had been served with an eviction order for non payment of rent. The church bell was rung, drawing hundreds of people to the scene. Five hundred members of the RIC, armed with rifles and swords marched from Portumna and joined with the two hundred troops of the Somerset Light to attempt to evict the family. There was strong resistance and the house became known as 'Saunders Fort'. The defenders threw boiling water, lime, rocks and beehives at the troops and police. After several hours the attackers withdrew. They were joined by reinforcements and finally succeeded in taking the house. Twenty two men were arrested during the encounter. On 12 September 1886 Fr Fahy, a local curate, was sent for trial for an alleged threat to J P Lewis of Ballingar House. He was sentenced to six months imprisonment. Following his trial on Fair Day, a further eighteen men were arrested. Around this period a process server, named Finlay, was shot dead in Woodford.

In October 1887 Wilfred Scawen Blunt, a prominent author, politician and agitator for the oppressed, was arrested when he organised a mass protest meeting. He was imprisoned for two months and gave an account of his experiences in *In Vinculis*.

The old Parochial Hall is now a Heritage Centre and the headquarters of the East Galway Family History Society, the designated centre for genealogical research in east Galway. Those searching for their roots in any of the thirty-five parishes in this area will find the centre an invaluable source of information.

RECOMMENDED

Woodford Mummers Feile (October).
Moran's Beer Garden.
Heritage Festival.
Heritage Centre.
1200 BC Stone Circle.
Ballynakill Wedge Tomb.
Poitín Stil Pub.
Derrycrag Wood.
St John the Baptist Catholic Church.
Ballynagar House.
Famine graveyard.
St Fechin's Well.
Marble Hill House.
East Galway Family History Society.
Tower-houses

Eyrecourt

Eyrecourt is an attractive, small village, ten miles north-east of Portumna, at the eastern boundary of County Galway. The village, situated in the Shannon Valley, is a popular centre with fishermen. The name in Irish is Dún an Uachta (the Fort of the Bank). There are a mixture of old and new buildings. Unfortunately many of the older houses are falling to ruin.

The village is named after the Eyre family. In 1651 Colonel John Eyre, a Cromwellian General, built a large house on the family estate. At the end of the eighteenth century, a descendant of his, George Eyre MP and Master of the hunt known as the Galway Blazers, was immortalised as the novelist's Charles Lever's 'Charles O'Malley'. The impressive gateway to the demesne is still standing. Over the years many distinguished guests visited the Eyres including Jonathan Swift, Charlotte Bronte and Arthur Guinness.

In 1203 when William de Burgo captured Connacht, he built a motte castle at Meelick, three miles south of Eyrecourt. From here de Burgo launched many attacks on vulnerable areas of the county. In 1229 his son, Richard, erected another castle at Meelick. In 1316, during hostilities, Felim O'Conor destroyed the castle. In 1479 Breasal O'Madden established a Franciscan abbey close to Richard de Burgo's castle. The abbey was dispersed during the Reformation and, although the friars returned, they were driven out again by Cromwellian troops.

About two miles north-east of Eyrecourt is Lismore Castle, built in the fifteenth century by the O'Madden family and once their principal seat. Through marriage the castle passed to the Burkes, and in turn to the Dalys of Dunsandle. Remains of the castle can still be seen today. In the 1700s Walter Lawrence erected a gateway at the entrance of Lissareaghaun House, to commemorate the Volunteers of the 1780s. The Lawrence family were descendants of a supporter of Sir John Perrot, who married one of the O'Maddens.

According to Samuel Lewis in his Topographical Dictionary of Ireland of 1837, the village contained 1789 inhabitants. He went on to record: 'This town, which takes its name from the Eyre family, lords of the manor, contains 342 houses, which are neat and well built. The market is on Saturday, and fairs are held on the Monday after Easter Monday, June 29, July 9, September 8, December 20 and one in October. Here are a court-house (in which quarter and petty sessions are held), gaol, and a constabulary police station; also the parish church, which is in bad repair and a RC chapel, built chiefly at the expense of C B Martin. A dispensary is supported in the usual way, and a decayed school-house is about to be restored by the Rev Mr Eyre, the incumbent of the parish.'

RECOMMENDED

Larry Duff's Pub.
Earner's.
Lynch's Farmhouse.
Lismore Castle.
McElroy's Pub.
Eyre House gateway.

There are a number of pubs in the village including Larry Duff's Pub, Earner's and McElroy's Pub, where the traveller can enjoy a quiet drink. Watch out for the shop with three names, General Supply Store on top of the building and at ground floor level the names O'Meara's and Donnellan's.

Portumna Castle (Jan de Fouw)

Portumna

Continuing north-eastwards from Woodford and following the course of the River Shannon, you will reach Portumna, a prosperous market town beside the north shore of Lough Derg, furthest down-river of the Shannon lakes. The name in Irish is Port Omna (the Landing Place of the Oak Tree). The surrounding countryside can be seen to best advantage from the highest point on Slieve Aughty Mountain, 1207 feet high. The town is an important base for cruising and fishing on the Shannon.

At the end of the twelfth century, William de Burgo acquired lands and built a stronghold in Portumna. In 1254 Richard de Cogan granted Portumna Priory, dedicated to St Peter and St Paul, to the Cistercian monks. In 1410 the priory was taken over by the Dominicans. Patrick Sarsfield married the daughter of the Earl of Clanrickard in the priory. The Portumna estates were originally the property of the O'Maddens and passed to the Clanrickard Burkes in the sixteenth century, when the heiress of Murchadh Óg O'Madden married Richard Mór MacWilliam. In 1609 the fourth Earl and Marquesses of Clanrickard built Portumna Castle, south of the town, with ornate grounds and deer parks. He spent much of the time at the English court. In July of that year the Earl was also granted a patent for a market on Tuesday and a fair on St Matthew's Day. There was a rent of 6*s* 8*d* for each market.

In 1634 the notorious Earl of Stafford held an inquisition at Portumna Castle to establish the title of the English Crown to the territory of Connacht. In 1641 the fifth Earl of Clanrickard returned to his castle during a period of unrest. In 1659 the castle was besieged by Cromwellian troops, under General Ludlow, who also attacked the Dominican Friary. In 1690 the Jacobite garrison in the castle surrendered to General Eppinger. Portumna Castle is now controlled by the Office of Public Works and is open to the public.

In 1643 Donal O'Madden built Derryhivenny Castle, three miles north of Portumna, one of the last tower houses built in Ireland. About six miles from the town on the Loughrea Road is Pallas Castle, built by the Burkes in the sixteenth century.

In 1797 Samuel Cox, an American, designed a wooden bridge which was erected across the River Shannon but, by the 1830s, the bridge was in poor condition and was replaced by a new bridge in 1841.

The last Marquess of Clanrickard was a landlord and miser. When he died, the direct line of the house of Mac William Uachtar Burke became extinct. The earldom passed to the Marquess of Sligo and the estates to the Earl of Harewood, who sold them. In 1826 the castle was accidently destroyed by fire. Later another castle, designed by Sir Thomas

Newenham Deane, was built on the same site. In 1922 during the Civil War the second castle was damaged by fire.

In the early 1830s the Grand Canal Company extended the canal to Portumna where the River Shannon enters Lough Derg. In 1836 over 4000 passengers used this section of the River from Portumna to Athlone. Today Portumna is an important juncture on the River Shannon with a modern marina for mooring.

Fr Thomas Burke, Parish Priest of Portumna and Mr Ryan, the resident Magistrate, succeeded in setting up a woollen factory where 110 girls were employed. In April 1848 the factory was forced to close due to lack of demand for their produce. During the evictions of 1886 the police and soldiers had their headquarters at Portumna and were practically boycotted by the locals. Traders were warned not to serve them. In 1889 there was one District Inspector, two Sergeants, one Acting Sergeant and twenty-one constables in Portumna barracks. Two of the constables were assigned to protect J Whelan, Clanrickard's estate agent.

Close to the town is Portumna Forest Park, consisting of 400 hectares of the Harewood estate, which is now under the control of the Forest and Wildlife Service. The park is a wildlife sanctuary, with an assortment of wildlife including red deer. The park also has nature trails and Lough Derg runs alongside its southern boundary. Sports enthusiasts are amply catered for with Portumna Golf Club and Tennis Club. The River Shannon offers excellent boating and angling facilities. The Emerald Star Line has about ninety cruisers for hire during the tourist season.

On the outskirts of the town the old workhouse lies in a bad state of repair. There are a number of industries in the town. Green Isle, the frozen food company, has increased its work force over the years. Another important employer is Mountain gate Data Systems.

For those seeking a snack, The Cup and Kettle Coffee Shop is to be recommended. For those seeking stronger refreshments, there is the Westpark Hotel or Clonwyn House Pub or The Boat House Bar.

RECOMMENDED

Portumna Forest Park.
Westpark Hotel.
Portumna Golf Club.
Portumna Castle.
Clonwyn House Pub.
Tourist Office.
Portumna Tennis Club.
Town Hall.
Lough Derg Drive.
Portumna Summer Festival (July).
The Boat House Bar.
The Cup and Kettle Coffee Shop.

Tynagh

The village of Tynagh, four miles north-west of Portumna, is in the centre of the parish of Tynagh, one of the largest parishes in the diocese of Clonfert. It is in the barony of Leitrim which is part of the ancient territory of Moenmagh, of the O'Nagtiteus and the O'Mullallys. The parish lies between the rivers Cappagh and Kilcrow. The name Tynagh in Irish is Tighneatha (The House of the Witch or The House of the Battle, as another source indicates). An earlier spelling of the name was Teena.

This small east Galway village, with two pubs and a population of about sixty people, gained national prominence in September 1993, with the visit of Paul Keating, Prime Minister of Australia. Mr Keating was visiting the birthplace of his great-great grandparents, John and Mary Keating, small tenant farmers in Tynagh, who were married in 1834. In 1855 after the potato famine, the Keatings and their eight children emigrated to Australia, travelling for six months. The Prime Minister's visit brought out a great pride in the community who took up paint and brushes to give the village a face-lift.

Three miles south-east of Tynagh, there is a burial ground called Cill Chorbáin, where the church of St Corban once stood. In medieval times the Dominicans built a priory at Cill Chorbáin. The priory has been partially restored and is worth a visit. In the fourteenth century Baron de Birmingham established a monastery for the Carmelites, close to the village. In 1589 the monastery was suppressed and no trace of it now remains.

Following the Anglo-Norman invasion, the de Burgos conquered the area and built Pallas Castle, south of Tynagh. In 1574 the castle was under the control of Jonyck Fitzthomas Burke, but following the restoration the building was granted to the Lords of Westmeath. The de Burgos (later Burkes) controlled the area until 1641. They built a manor house beside the castle. In Cromwellian times Pallas Castle was granted to the Nugents, Earls of Westmeath, upon their transportation to Connacht. The youngest Nugent brother, took the title Riverston. King James II appointed Thomas Nugent to the position of Chief Justice of the King's bench in Ireland.

In 1851 Anthony Francis Nugent dropped the title Riverston. In time the Nugent family came to own most of the land in the parish of Tynagh. When the last member died, unmarried, in the 1930s, the Land Commission bought the remaining estate and its mansion. They demolished the mansion and divided the land among the farmers.

The old Catholic church in Tynagh was a reconstructed barn which was first used in 1764. In 1971 the new parish church of St Laurence was

RECOMMENDED

Harney's Pub.
Gordon's Pub.
Tynagh Horse Show.
Community Centre.
Cill Chorbáin.
Pallas Castle.

built and dedicated. There was once a Church of Ireland church in the village but no sign of it remains today. In an ancient graveyard named Billow, east of the village, stands a tree, reputed to have magical powers.

About a half a mile north of the village lies the site of the Tynagh Mines which in the 1960s and 70s was the richest lead and zinc mine in Europe. Up to 500 people were employed in the mines, until they closed in the early 1980s when they were worked out. The closure had a devastating effect on the community but, with their resilience, locals established a number of small industries.

The visit of Mr Keating gave the Tynagh and District Development Association the incentive to try and attract tourists to the village. They plan to turn the old school house into a heritage centre and museum. Tynagh has traditionally been the home of good hurlers with a number of the 1923 winning All-Ireland team coming from the village. Harney's Pub has a display of the life and times of Tynagh hurling on the walls. There is also a good deal of equestrian activity in the area, which includes an indoor riding school and pony trekking holidays. The village only has two pubs, Gordon's and Harney's, both of which are worth a visit. The village's thatched house is well preserved.

Clonfert

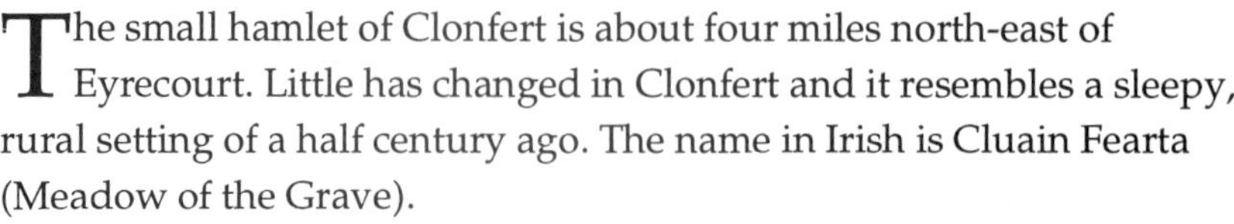

The small hamlet of Clonfert is about four miles north-east of Eyrecourt. Little has changed in Clonfert and it resembles a sleepy, rural setting of a half century ago. The name in Irish is Cluain Fearta (Meadow of the Grave).

In 563 a monastery was built in Clonfert by St Brendan the Navigator and a monastic community grew around it. There is evidence that, when the Vikings invaded Ireland in the eighth century, they attacked Clonfert. According to the *Annals of Ulster* the church at Clonfert was one of many burned in 748. In 838 Feidhlimidh, King of Cashel attacked the monks at Clonfert and seized the abbacies. It was attacked and destroyed on a number of other occasions and subsequently rebuilt.

In 1164 Turlough O'Conor, King of Connacht, at St Malachy's suggestion, built Clonfert Cathedral for the Augustinian Canons Regular. The cathedral is renowned for its elaborate west doorway, one of the finest examples of Hiberno-Romanesque to be found in the country. The bishop resided in a house close to the cathedral. This house was later owned by Sir Oswald Mosley, leader of the British Union of Fascists. In 1950 the house was burned down but was later repaired.

A short distance from the cathedral, past the crossroads, is Our Lady of Clonfert Catholic Church. Inside the church, there is a carved wooden statue of the Virgin and Child, dating to the fourteenth century. Close to the church is one of the many keep castles in south Galway. Two fields beyond the cathedral is Emmanuel House of Providence. This complex has a small oratory and organises work camps for young people from abroad.

Far left: Mermaid in Clonfert cathedral
Left: Doorway in Clonfert cathedral

RECOMMENDED

St Brendan's Cathedral.
Emmanuel House of Providence.
Our Lady of Clonfert Catholic Church.
Keep Castle.

Craughwell

Craughwell is a small, village on the main Dublin-Galway Road. According to PW Joyce in *Irish Names for Places*, the name Creachmhaoil means 'A Place of Plunders'. Other sources give the translation of Creamhchaoil as 'Wild Garlic Wood.'

About two miles from Craughwell, on the Athenry Road, are the ruins of Moyode Castle. In the 1770s, at Moyode Castle, the Persse family, along with the Persses of Roxoboro, established their own pack of foxhounds and found the renowned Galway Blazers. The Kennels of the Galway Blazers used the village as their headquarters and some hunts still commence from there. Lady Augusta Gregory (a key figure in the Irish Literary Revival movement) was a member of the Persse family. During the 1916 Rising, Moyode Castle was occupied by Liam Mellowes and other Volunteers from Galway.

In 1823 Anthony Daly, a local man, was hanged for attempting to murder Mr Burke, the landlord. Since the hanging, no grass has grown on the location of the execution, on the outskirts of the village.

In 1820 Robert O'Hara-Burke, the explorer and the first person to cross Australia from south to west, was born in St Cleran's, a Georgian mansion, close to the village. A later occupant of the house was the distinguished American film director, John Huston, who lived here for many years from the early 1960s. He became Master of the Galway Blazers and entertained many international guests at his home including Montgomery Clift, Marlon Brando and Katherine Hepburn. Huston attempted to establish an Irish film industry and directed some major films on location in Ireland including *Moby Dick, Sinful Davey, The List of Adrian Messanger* and *The Mackintosh Man*. His daughter, Anjelica, the Oscar winning film actress, spent much of her childhood at St Cleran's. Anjelica's brother, Tony, now a film director and screenwriter also lived there as a child.

Antoine Ó Reachtabhra (Antoine Raftery), better known as Blind Raftery, the celebrated blind poet, was born in County Mayo in 1784 but spent much of his life in the vicinity of Craughwell. He wandered the roads, composing poems for the poor and on topical events of the day. When he died on Christmas Eve in 1835, he was buried in nearby Killora graveyard. On the green in the village, statues have been erected by the community to honour Raftery and Lady Gregory. Both statues are by the sculptor Donal O'Murhcadha. Early this century there were disturbances near Craughwell in which a police constable, named McGoldrick, was shot dead. Craughwell also has a fine tradition of hurling and one of her favourite sons, Dick Morrissey, won an All-Ireland medal, playing for Galway in 1924.

RECOMMENDED

St Colman's Catholic Church.
Cheever's Pub.
Raftery's statue.
Lady Gregory's statue.
Rahasane Turlough Wildlife Reserve.
Raftery's Pub.
Cawley's Pub.

Loughrea

Loughrea is a market town on the main Ballinasloe to Galway Road. The town takes its name from a small lake on the northern shores, Baile Locha Riach (the Town of Grey Lake). South of the town are the Slieve Aughty Mountains and a numbers of crannógs in Lough Rea.

The town is particularly noted for its brightly coloured houses and shops. It must hold the Irish record with thirty-five pubs in the main street. There are five public parks and a swimming area at the eastern end of the town. Within walking distance of the town centre reminders of its medieval history still survive.

In 1236 Richard de Burgo, the Norman adventurer, received grants of land in Connacht and established a Norman stronghold in Loughrea. He built walls around the town and was responsible for its subsequent development, despite carrying out a ruthless war of colonisation in the area. The de Burgos later became known as the Burkes and later still the Earls of Clanrickards. In 1300 the de Burgos founded a Carmelite Friary in the town, which in later times held the tombs of old Loughrea families. At the suppression of the monasteries, the Friary was granted to the Earl of Clanrickard.

In 1585 the jail of the newly created County of Galway was established in the centre of Loughrea. The judges of assize recommended the Grand Jury to build a new jail in Galway and that all prisoners should be transported from Loughrea jail, which was 'so old and ruinous'. Loughrea jail closed in 1674.

In 1605 a patent was granted for a fair to be held in Loughrea on May Day. In later years, more regular fairs and markets were held in the town.

By the early 1800s there was a constabulary police stationed in Loughrea. It was the chief station and revenue headquarters for Athlone and most of County Galway. A court house was opened and a Mr Fahy established a brewery. Cotton spinning was another small industry in the town. The Church of Ireland church was erected in 1821 with a loan from the Board of First Fruits. In 1832 the spire was struck by lightning and crashed onto the roof.

In 1837 Samuel Lewis in his *Topographical Dictionary of Ireland* gave the following description of Loughrea: 'It at present consists of several streets, and contains 1229 houses, of which many are neat and well built. There is a promenade called the Mall, which is much frequented, and the neighbourhood abounds with pleasingly diversified scenery. The lake, which is about one mile wide, has three small islands of picturesque appearance, and its shores are enlivened by some pleasing cottages, and embellished on the south and east with hills of beautiful verdure.'

The workhouse built for £7000 to accommodate 800 people, received its first paupers on 24 March 1842. When additional space was required, the old brewery was taken over and converted into dormitories. Up to 1127 paupers were housed there. Edward Martyn, the wealthy Catholic landlord, poet and playwright, lived in Loughrea at Mason Brook House, for a period in the mid 1850s. He went on to write such plays as *The Heather Field, Maeve* and *A Tale of a Town.*

In 1886 Michael Davitt addressed a large Land League meeting in the town. In November of that year Clanrickard's tenants met in Loughrea and formed a central committee, to pursue a 'No Rent' campaign.

Loughrea is the cathedral town of the Catholic diocese of Clonfert. St Brendan's Cathedral, an imposing building, designed by William Byrne was built between 1897-1903, to succeed St Brendan's Cathedral in Clonfert. The building displays an array of ecclesiastical art in Ireland between 1903-57. There are stained glass windows by Sarah Purser and other members of her Tower of Glass. John Hughes sculpted the Virgin

Bottom left: Loughrea cathedral banner
Bottom right: Loughrea cathedral

RECOMMENDED

Loughrea Cathedral.
Loughrea Co-op.
GAA Museum.
Loughrea Golf Club.
Arch Bar (Music).
Old Town Gate.
Loughrea Horse Show (July).
Temperance Hall (Bingo Mon).
Ringo's Nite Club.
The Lantern Bar.
Loughrea Tennis Club.
Aille Cross Equestrian Centre.
Diocesan Museum.
Loughrea Literary and Historical Society.
Turoe Pet Farm and Leisure Park (April - October)

and Child statue and other works are by Evie Hone, A E Childe and Michael Healy. Some were also designed by Jack B Yeats. Close to the cathedral is the fifteenth century gate, which still stands. In the cathedral grounds the Diocesan Museum displays liturgical artefacts and primitive statues, which survived the repression of the Penal Days.

Three miles north of Loughrea, at Ballaun, is the Turoe Stone, a three foot high rounded granite pillar with a swirling mass of opposing spirals, La Tène style. Experts date the stone to the first century AD. Also in the vicinity is a megalithic structure known as the Seven Mountains, consisting of seven stones in a low circular bank close to a square chamber tomb. There are two ringforts at Rahannagroagh and Rathsonny.

Seamus O'Kelly was born in Loughrea in 1881 and became a reporter on a local paper. He was involved in the revolutionary movement and went on to distinguish himself as a writer, and produced plays, novels and short stories. His best known works were his novella, *The Weaver's Grave* and his collection of stories *By the Stream of Kilmeen*. In 1918 Kelly was Arthur Griffith's deputy and died of a heart attack on 14 November that year.

For football fans the museum in Dunkellin Street, which traces the history of the GAA, is worth a visit. Sporting enthusiasts of all tastes are catered for in Loughrea, which has a tennis club, an eighteen hole golf course, several equestrian centres and excellent angling on the lake and many rivers. The town is also noted for its strong traditional music heritage and music sessions can frequently be enjoyed, especially in the Arch Bar.

East Galway

The area which I have termed east Galway is bordered on the west by Lough Corrib and extends northwards to the County Mayo border, eastwards to the County Roscommon border and its southern boundary is the Ballinasloe to Galway Road. The average Irish visitor or foreign tourist will list Galway City and Connemara on their agenda but will miss out on this uncluttered and generally uncommercial region. Few travel books do justice to the heritage and amenities of the area. East Galway can modestly boast of many places of historical, religious and cultural significance: from the festive Ballinasloe Horse Show Fair to Dunmore Castle and Friary to the scenes of the bloody battles of Athenry and Aughrim. This latter battle is re-enacted in the Interpretative Centre. Commence the tour of this section at Claregalway and continue northwards through the mainly flat, rich farming land to the angler's delights of Annaghdown and Headford. Then zig-zag eastwards to Tuam, with its twin cathedrals. Next proceed northwards to the historic village of Milltown and then due east to the crossroads of Glenamaddy, famed in song, before continuing south through the attractive villages of Moylough and Mount Bellew back to Ballinasloe.

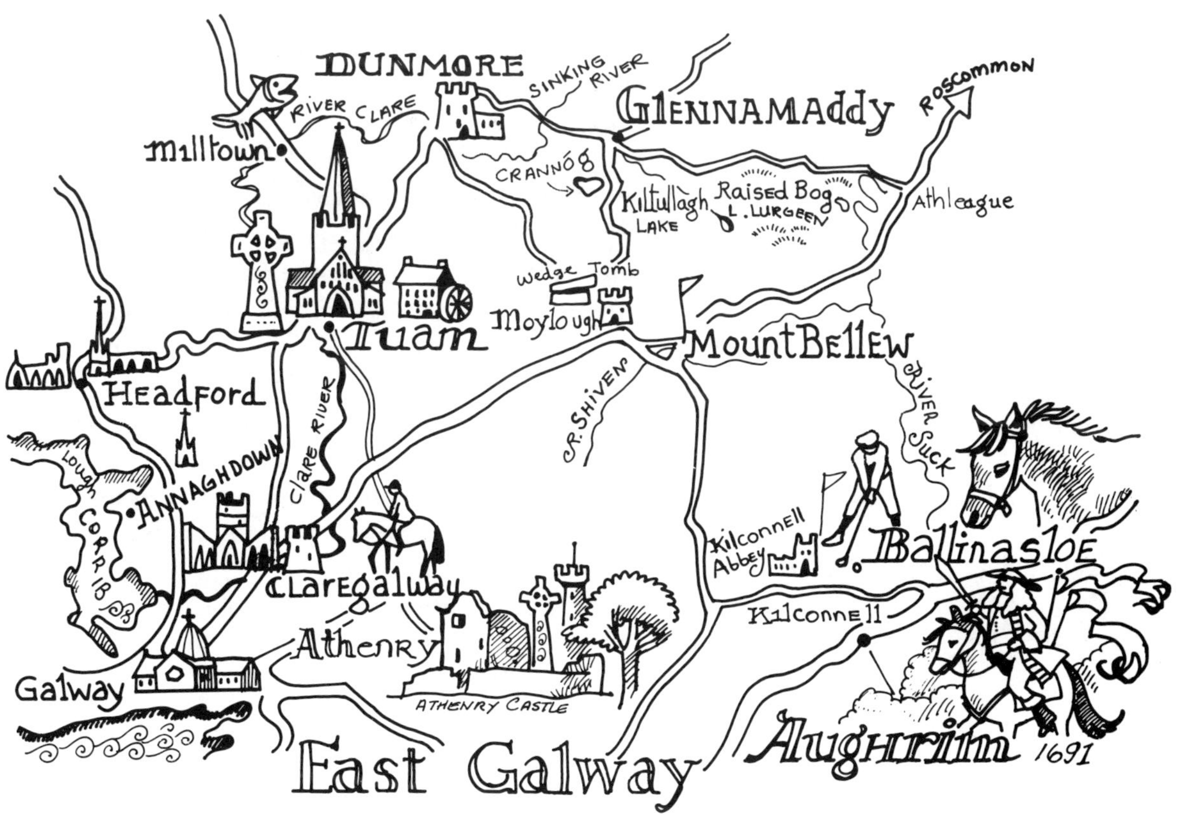

Claregalway

RECOMMENDED

Pony Trekking.
Franciscan Friary.
Claregalway Castle.
Malachy Hession's Pub.
Dunleavy's Lounge.
Nine Arches Bar.
Catholic Church of Assumption and St James.

The small village of Claregalway is located where the Galway to Tuam Road crosses the Claregalway River. Claregalway in Irish means Baile 'n Chláir (the Town of the Palin or Flat Down). Earlier references mention it as Clar an Diabhail (Devil's Flat) because, according to tradition, at this juncture the river was crossed on planks supported by pillars.

Above the river, which is noted for its excellent salmon fishing are the ruins of Claregalway Castle. For a village of its size, Claregalway has got more than its quota of good pubs, among them Nine Arches Bar, Dunleavy's Lounge and Malachy Hession's Pub. For the more agile, there is pony trekking in the village.

In 1290 John de Cogan built the Franciscan Friary at Clare-ya-dowl, with an eighty foot tower. Beside the ruins of the friary, is a burial ground. In 1867 Sir William Wilde wrote; 'It is said, under the date of 1296, that Philip de Blund, Archdeacon of Tuam, during the time of the dispute respecting the episcopacy of Enachdun, took by violence from the friars of Clare-Galway, in which place they had been deposited, the pontificarlia, consisting of the chest containing the "episcopal mitre", together with the pastoral staff, and sundry other things, "of the neighbouring cathedral".' In the fifteenth century the friary was renovated and the tower was added. Following the suppression, Henry VIII granted the friary to Richard de Burgo. The Franciscans were expelled on numerous occasions, but kept returning and resided there until 1765.

In the fifteenth century the de Burgos built a castle, with a sixty-five foot tower, beside the river crossing and it became an important stronghold, preventing the movement of troops and supplies. In 1504, at Knockdoe, five miles north of Claregalway, Gearóid Mór, Earl of Kildare, assisted by some of the Irish princes, defeated Ulick III of Clanrickard and his allies. In 1538 Lord Deputy Grey, with the support of artillery, succeeded in taking Claregalway Castle. In the rebellion of 1641, the castle was garrisoned by troops of the Marquess of Clanrickard. Two years later, it was captured by the Burkes for the Confederates. In 1651 the castle was again taken, on this occasion, by Sir Charles Coote, a Cromwellian officer.

Like so many other areas of County Galway, the Volunteers were active during Easter Week 1916. A number of local Volunteers attacked an RIC patrol near the village, killing one constable.

CLAREGALWAY ABBEY

Annaghdown

Turn left off the Headford Road at Corandulla crossroads and continue towards Lough Corrib until you reach the small village of Annaghdown, on the shore of the lake. The name in Irish is Eanach Dhúin (Marsh of the Fort). The old passenger steamer pier is now the base for a waterbus and angling craft. Boats can be hired at the pier to bring passengers fishing or to view the small wooded islands on the lake. Close by is a popular swimming area.

Legend has it that in the sixth century, St Brendan the Navigator founded a monastery at Annaghdown and was abbot there until he died in 577. He was buried in Clonfert. It is believed that St Brigid, his sister, established a convent at Annaghdown and resided there for a period.

In the twelfth century the monastery was taken over by the Canons Regular of St Augustine but is reputed to have been dissolved a century later. In 1188 Annaghdown became the see of a new diocese, covering the jurisdiction of the O'Flaherty territory, east of the lake. In 1195 the Augustinian Sisters from Arrouaise in France, established St Mary's convent nearby. In 1325 when Annaghdown became permanently under the control of the archdiocese of Tuam the English of Galway came under the unwanted influence of the Irish.

The cathedral at Annaghdown was built in the thirteenth century. Later the building served as a Church of Ireland church for the parish. West of the cathedral are priory remains. In the vicinity are St Brendan's Well and St Corman's Well and a fifteenth century tower house, overlooking the bay.

The area is well established in Irish folk memory due to the poem, *Anach Cuain*, by Antoine Raftery, lamenting a tragic drowning in 1828. About thirty members of the local community, with their belongings and ten sheep, set off in an old boat to travel the eight miles to the fair in Galway. One of the sheep put its hoof through the bottom of the boat and it sprung a leak. A man attempted to plug the hole with his coat but pushed out the plank. Within seconds all the people were in the water, and, although close to land, nineteen of them were drowned, eleven men and eight women. There is a marble memorial to commemorate the tragedy.

RECOMMENDED

Castle.
Lough Corrib.
Waterbus.
Tower House.
St Brendan's Cathedral.
St Brendan's Well.
St Cormac's Well.

Headford

The town of Headford is situated on the Galway to Ballinrobe Road. The name Headford means, Ath Cinn (the Ford Head or the Ford of the Peak). According to Richard Hayward in *The Corrib Country*, it is The Ford of the Son of Cing. Headford is a reasonable size market town and a good angling centre, adjacent to Lough Corrib. There are miles of stone walls, much associated with County Galway, in the vicinity. The town has won many awards in the Bord Fáilte Tidy Towns Competition, as is evident from the attractive façades of the business premises. The town is tidy and clean but lacking in atmosphere.

Two miles west of Headford are the remains of Killfhursa (Church of Fursa), which is believed to have been built by St Fursey, a follower of St Brendan, circa 620. Fursey was a celebrated Irish saint and traveller and the patron saint of the O'Flahertys.

Prior to the Anglo-Norman invasion, the O'Flahertys held the land around Headford. On Knockma, the only hill for some distance, is a Norman castle, which, according to legend, was the home of King Finbar and his Connacht fairies. Another local tradition states that Queen Maeve, the mythical Queen of Connacht was buried on the hill. For a panoramic view of the surrounding coutryside climb to the summit. There is a cairn here and nearby is Finbar's Castle.

In 1351 a Franciscan Friary, called Ross Errilly Abbey, was founded by Sir Raymond de Burgo on the banks of the Black River, close to the village. The friary was renovated in 1470 and granted to the Earls of Clanrickard who sheltered the friars when they were being suppressed. The friars returned many times to the abbey between 1538 and 1753. In 1596 the friary was captured by the British and became a garrison. In 1656 it was damaged by Cromwellian troops but was later repaired.

In 1688 Sir Thomas Molyneux, a physician and antiquarian, gave an account of a swarm of locusts which invaded the area: 'From hence they made their way into the more inland parts, towards Headford, a place belonging to Sir George St George Bart. Here, and in the adjacent country, multitudes of them showed themselves among the trees and hedges in the day-time, hanging by the boughs; thousands together, in clusters, sticking to the back one of another, as in the manner of bees when they swarm. Towards evening they would all rise, disperse and fly about, with a strong humming noise, and in such vast, incredible numbers, that they darkened the air for the space of two or three miles square.'

Close to Headford is Castlehacket, a Georgian mansion, built by the Kirwan family in 1703. In 1822 the building was destroyed by fire but it was later rebuilt.

Early in the nineteenth century a ringfort called Cahergal was displaced to make way for a new police barracks. In 1826 Mary Kelly, the poet, who wrote *Eva of the Nation*, was born in Headford. She married the Young Irelander, Kevin O'Doherty.

In 1837 Samuel Lewis in his *Topographical Dictionary of Ireland*, gave the following account of Headford: 'This is a neat and clean town, having been much improved by its proprietor R J Manseragh St George; it has considerable trade, and commands fine views of Lough Corrib, and the mountains of Joyce's Country and Mayo. It comprises 217 houses, containing 1441 inhabitants, a chief constabulary police station, Petty Sessions, dispensary; bobbin lace, coarse linen and flannel are made. Headford Castle, residence of R J M St George was erected on ruins of an ancient castle.'

Like so many other rural towns there are many pubs worth visiting including Varley's, The White Horse Inn, McHugh's and The Thatch Pub. For appetising food the Anglers' Rest Hotel could not be surpassed.

RECOMMENDED

Ross Errilly Abbey.
The Thatch Pub.
Killfursa Church.
Headford Hall (occasional ceilis).
Anglers' Rest Hotel.
Varley's.
The White Horse Inn.
McHugh's.

Below: Ross Errilly Abbey (Office of Public Works)

Tuam

The town of Tuam is situated about thirteen miles east of Headford and is the principal town of north Galway. The name Tuam in Irish is Tuaim Dá Ghualann, meaning 'Tumulus (or ridge) of the Two Shoulders'.

The town is still an important industrial and agricultural centre for mid-Connacht and was once a thriving, vibrant town before the closing of the Erin Foods factory and the cutting back of the Digital workforce. For approximately 1500 years Tuam has been a major ecclesiastical see and the ecclesiastical capital of Connacht, with both a Catholic and Church of Ireland cathedral. One of the country's four Catholic Archbishops has his seat there.

Recent improvements in the town centre have smartened up its appearance. New pavements have been laid and ornate railings have been erected. One important landmark which has been removed is the ancient stone cross. It stood in a precarious position in the centre of the square and is now in St Mary's Cathedral. The library staff are most helpful for those seeking local history information and the relevant books.

In the fifth century St Jarlath, a disciple of St Benignus, founded a monastery and school at Cluanfois, west of Tuam. The monastery gained a scholastic reputation and among those who studied there was St Brendan the Navigator. There is a legend that Jarlath came to Tuam following a dream which St Brendan interpreted for him. The dream informed him that he should leave Cluanfois and establish a new monastery if his chariot wheel should break. The incident occurred at Tuaim Dá Ghualann and since then Tuam's symbol has been a broken chariot wheel. Jarlath is the patron saint of the archdiocese of Tuam.

In 1049 following his defeat of the O'Flahertys, Aedh O'Connor turned Tuam into a fortress and established his residence there, making the town a royal capital. The O'Connors continued to hold power in Connacht and in 1106 Turlough O'Connor became King of Connacht. Twelve years later Turlough O'Connor had become High King of Ireland and, for a period in the twelfth century, Tuam was the capital of Ireland. In 1152 O'Connor and Archbishop Hessian of Tuam built the Cathedral of St Mary in the town and, following the Synod of Kells, it became the seat of the Archbishop.

By the time of the Anglo-Norman invasion in 1235, Tuam had been firmly established as an ecclesiastical centre. In the town's market place stood an early twelfth century high ringed sandstone cross, fourteen feet high, with inscriptions in memory of Ó Hóisín (Hessian), the abbot, who became Archbishop of Tuam and Turlough O'Connor. The cross was

Left and below: Tuam High Cross

partly built from rocks found in the graveyard. Richard de Burgo was granted the confiscated lands of the O'Connors and, under his patronage, there was steady growth in the town.

In 1613 King James I granted a charter to the town specifying a layout, which had the main roads converging on the town square (in fact it is diamond shaped). In 1645 Sir Charles Coote, in his march to capture Sligo, attacked the town and killed the titular archbishop.

Four miles north of Tuam is Tollendal Castle, the ancestral home of the Lally family. One of the family became the great French general, Baron de Lally, who was executed by King Louis XV but, later his name was inscribed on the Arc de Triomphe in Paris. One mile east of the castle, on the Dunmore Road, is the largest of the earthworks in the district.

By the late 1700s Tuam was a bustling market town with regular markets held in Market Square which attracted dealers and travellers from all over east and north Galway. In 1778 the army barracks was built, followed in quick succession by a court house and jail. Between 1827-37 the Catholic Cathedral of the Assumption was constructed. It was a perpendicular style building with a square tower, designed in the gothic style by Dominic Madden. There are some unique stone faces sculpted on the cathedral. Beside the cathedral are the remains of Temple Jarlath, dating from circa 1360. In 1834 Archbishop John McHale was appointed to Tuam. He was a staunch supporter of the Irish language and was one of the most eminent church leaders of the nineteenth century.

In 1842 William Makepeace Thackeray gave his assessment of the town in his *Irish Sketchbook*: 'I had the pleasure of inspecting a very mouldy dirty town and made my way to the Catholic Cathedral - a very handsome edifice indeed; handsome without and within, and of the Gothic sort. Over the door is a huge coat of arms, surmounted by a Cardinal's hat - the arms of the See, no doubt, quartered with John Tuam's own patrimonial coat; and that was a frieze coat, from all accounts, passable and ragged at the elbow.'

From the mid-1850s Tuam had many sporting organisations. The Tuam Cricket Club consisted of members of the gentry. The Annual Race Meeting was the social event of the year. The vast majority of the people lived in small dwellings and worked the land for minimal wages. A workhouse was built on the Dublin Road and gave shelter to the poor of the district. The only railway line in North Galway was the Athenry to Claremorris line which passed through the town. For the most part, horse-drawn cars and bicycles were the mode of transport. Plays were performed in the Town Hall, along with shows by touring companies and Grand Concerts were staged on Sunday nights. The popular Charles Cook's travelling group played regularly at this venue. Between 1861-78 the new Church of Ireland Cathedral of St Marys was built to a design by Sir Thomas Deane, incorporating a portion of the earlier cathedral. The most striking features of the building are the stained glass windows and the church arch.

On 29 May 1884 Charles Stewart Parnell visited Tuam unexpectedly, accompanied by John Philip Nolan MP and Captain Willie O'Shea. A large crowd greeted them at the station. Parnell formed a company called 'The Irish Land Purchase and Settlement Company Limited'. In 1892 at an open-air anti-Parnellite rally, opponents and supporters of Parnell clashed in the town. When anti-Parnellites attempted to drag speakers from the platform, sticks, stones and cudgels were used in the attack. The fracas only broke up when the crowd was baton charged by the police.

During the 1880s the Rishworth family who ran a timber mill in the town, established a match factory which employed many local girls. In 1897 an American, who stayed in the town, gave the following description of the travelling population: 'a motley crowd of itinerants, musicians, ballad-singers, flute-players, pipers, fiddlers, cornet-players and others too numerous to mention blowing vigorously in a kind of discordant rivalry. "Yes," a gentleman of the town said to me, "they all find their way to Tuam." It is a sort of headquarters of every tramp giving the road who, no doubt, looks upon it as a haven of rest and a valley of tears.'

In July 1920 two RIC constables were ambushed and shot dead close to Tuam. In further attacks the Town Hall was gutted and the RIC barracks was badly damaged. In 1922 the workhouse barracks came under repeated attack. In April 1923, during the Civil War, six Republican prisoners were brought from Galway to Tuam and were executed in the old workhouse by Free State troops. Their bodies were taken to Athlone but in 1924 they were returned to Tuam for burial in their native place.

In 1933 a new era dawned for Tuam when the Taoiseach, Eamon deValera, turned the first sod on the construction of the Sugar Factory. The plant opened in 1934 and not alone created employment but gave an economic boost to the surrounding farming community. There was a subsequent influx of workers to the town which led to the Town Commissioners building several new housing estates. In later years the plant became known as Erin Foods and in 1970 an extension was added. The 1980s was to be a troubled period for Erin Foods and the factory closed making hundreds unemployed.

Two of the most distinguished names to be associated with Tuam, in recent years, have been Tom Murphy, the playwright, and the group, The Sawdoctors. Murphy was born in Tuam in 1936. As a young man he taught metal work for a number of years and was involved with the

RECOMMENDED

Mill Museum.
St Mary's Cathedral.
The Imperial Hotel.
Catholic Cathedral of the Assumption.
St Jarlath's College.
High Cross Pub.
The Hare Inn.
High Cross.

Tuam Theatre Guide. Following the success of his first play *On the Outside* (which he co-wrote with Noel O'Donoghue) he became a full-time playwright and wrote such critically acclaimed plays as *The Sanctuary Lamp*, *The Gigli Concert* and *Bailegangaire*. He became a director of the Abbey Theatre, where most of his plays were produced. Within a short span of time, The Sawdoctors have become a household name throughout Ireland with their succession of hit records and albums which include*If this is Rock and Roll*, *I Want my Old Job Back* and *All the Way from Tuam*. They attract capacity crowds to their many Irish and worldwide concerts and pay their annual visit to the Galway Arts Festival.

Those with some time to spare could pass away a few peaceful hours visiting the two cathedrals and Mill Museum and partaking of a meal in The Imperial Hotel or a jar in one of the many pubs including The Hare Inn or High Cross Pub.

TUAM CATHEDRAL

Athenry

Athenry is a thirteenth century medieval walled town, in the heart of rich farming country, off the main Ballinasloe to Galway Road. Its name in Irish, Baile Átha an Ri (Town of the King's Ford) devolves from its position at the junction of the three ancient kingdoms of Hy-Many (O Kelly), Hy-Briuin Seola (O'Flaherty) and Hy-Fiachrach (O'Hynes). The ford refers to the Clareen River which flows through the town.

The narrow meandering streets, with their bright shop fronts and pubs, merge with the remains of the town's ancient past. Within the town and its environs there are many examples of its heritage with ruins of walls, tower gates, the fifteenth century market cross, castles and ancient churches.

Following the Anglo-Norman invasion, the de Burgos conquered much of Connacht in 1235. They granted the area around Athenry to Meiler de Bermingham second Baron of Athenry, who established the town and surrounded it with a curtain wall with towers and a moat. He fortified it as his centre of power in Galway and in 1238 he erected Athenry Castle with a surrounding lawnwall, with two corner towers. The castle was also known as Bermingham Castle and King John's Castle. The castle has been recently restored and is open to the public.

In 1241 Meiler de Bermingham founded St Peter and St Paul's Friary for the Dominican Order. The building of the friary took twenty years to complete. When de Bermingham died in 1252 he was buried in the friary. The building was accidentally destroyed by fire in 1423 but was later rebuilt and was burned again in 1574. Several members of the Bermingham family are buried in the friary.

In 1280 St Mary's Parish Church was built in the town. In 1484 it became Collegiate by order of the Archbishop of Tuam. In 1576 the institution was suppressed and burned by Clanrickard's sons (their mother was interred in the church). In 1828 the spire was added.

On 10 August 1316, a battle was fought, close to the town, between Phelim O'Connor, King of Connacht, his ally, the Prince of Thomond, and the Anglo-Normans, William de Burgo and Richard de Bermingham. O'Connor and his men put up a vigorous defence against the bowmen but were finally defeated. Phelim and sixty Irish lords were among the 8000 killed. With the spoils of battle De Burgo built sturdier walls around the town. He also added a wide outer moat and six wall towers, some of which still remain today. In 1324 de Burgo had the church rebuilt but it was burned on several occasions. In the fourteenth century Thomas de Bermingham commissioned an ornate silver crucifixion for the church. Cromwellian forces closed the church in 1652.

In 1499 Wadim, a wealthy landlord, became a patron of the

Dominican priory. During the fifteenth century a cross head, with a crucifixion on one side and the Virgin and Child on the reverse, was erected in the town's market place.

In 1577, the town, then an outpost of Galway, was attacked by 'Mic an Iarla', the sons of the Earl of Clanrickard. Three years later the town was attacked again and the buildings and walls were damaged. In 1575 a charter was granted, ordering that a common clerk should be appointed to the town. The charter also stated that a fair was to be held in Athenry from the Eve of St John's Day (23 June) to the feast of St Thomas (3 July) the Martyr. The town was to have a pillory and ducking stool. The provost, in directing their use, was to obtain the counsel of four burgesses in different cases. In 1596 the town was sacked by Red Hugh O'Donnell.

Two miles south-west of Athenry is Moyode Castle, an ancient and ruined mansion. In 1770 the nucleus of what was to become the Galway Blazers Foxhounds was formed here. Athenry also became the headquarters of the County Galway Cricket Club. South-west of Athenry are the ruins of the fifteenth century Derrydonnell Castle.

At the end of the nineteenth century Athenry became an important railway junction where the Dublin to Galway and Limerick to Sligo lines crossed. The town held traditional fairs and markets. In January 1888 Wilfred Blunt, an English poet and radical, was arrested for holding a public meeting about evictions and was imprisoned for three months. There was a large demonstration at Athenry station in his favour.

In June 1914 Volunteers from all over Galway gathered at Athenry where the first County Galway Volunteer review was held. In Easter week 1916 Liam Mellowes and his colleagues took over Moyode Castle for several days and had an engagement with the RIC nearby.

About three miles north of Athenry, on the Tuam Road, is the (occupied) Lambert mansion, known as Castle Ellen. Isabella Lambert, mother of Sir Edward Carson, who armed the Ulster Volunteer Force (UVF), was born here. Pádraic Fallon was an important figure born in Athenry in 1905. He became a customs and excise official in Dublin where he began his literary career. He wrote short stories, radio drama and poetry. He died in 1974.

Today there is a busy cattle and sheep mart in the town and also a horse fair. Mellowes Agricultural College provides training and research facilities for young farmers.

A new amenity in the area is The Fields of Athenry Heritage Cottage and Museum. The recreated traditional Irish cottage evokes a period when such a home was a focus for family and neighbours who gathered to listen to a seanachai (story-teller) or music. Athenry is now a recognised heritage town, a coveted distinction.

Monivea is a small village approximately seven miles north-east of

RECOMMENDED

Athenry Castle.
Dominican Friary.
Old walls.
Dunclarin Arms.
Clarin River.
Point-to-Point (April).
Monivea Forest Trek.
The Fields of Athenry Thatched Cottage and Museum.
Athenry Festival (August).
Queen of Athenry (August).
Golf Club.
Lady's Well.

Athenry and is one of the best examples of a landlord-planned town in Ireland. The village is noted for the width of its street and wide greens. There are three castles within a short radius of the village, Killaclogher Castle, Clonbrush Castle and one in the demesne of the former Ffrench (an ancient Galway tribal family) estate. In 1900 the Ffrench family built a mausoleum on their estate and on the death of Cathleen Ffrench the lands were given to the state. There are pleasant forest walks with the River Killaclogher running nearby.

Far right: North Gate
Right: Athenry Castle, known locally as King John's Castle
Below: Dominican Priory, Athenry (Michael Melia)

Kilconnell

RECOMMENDED
O'Donnellan Monument.
Broderick's Bar (Traditional music).
Franciscan Friary ruins.

The small village of Kilconnell is about three miles north-west of Aughrim. The name Kilconnell in Irish is Cill Chonaill (Conall's Church). In the sixth century it was believed that St Conall and a group of monks built a church here and the area has retained the name of Cill Chonaill (the Church of Conall). In medieval times the village was known as Cill-Conainne. Conall had to seek permission from the chieftain who controlled the Barony of Kilconnell to establish his church.

In 1353 William O'Kelly, Lord of Hy Many, founded an abbey for Conventual Franciscans on the site of St Conall's church. In 1460 the abbey was reformed by his son Malachy, and at the dissolution it was granted to Charles Calthorpe, an English settler. In the late sixteenth century Queen Elizabeth I held the abbey and a British garrison was stationed there. In 1651 Major Dermot O'Daly successfully defended the friary against the Cromwellians. In an edict of King William, the monks were ordered to leave by January 1698. They obeyed and vacated the abbey and were protected by local landlords during the Penal Days.

In the north wall of the abbey's nave there are two tomb chests. The west tomb has figures of St John, St Mary and St James. According to tradition, in 1691 after the Battle of Aughrim, St Ruth, leader of the Irish against King William, was buried here. It was a favourite burial ground for many of the respected families of Galway.

In the 1830s three members of the White family were publically hanged in the village for activities against the Crown. In 1836 there was a population of 1910 in the village. That same year 170 children were being educated in three private schools. The remainder of the children were attending hedge schools. A number of fairs were held annually in the village.

Kilconnell was quick to respond to the Gaelic revival movement and in 1895 young men formed a hurling team. They made their own hurleys and sliotars (hurling balls). There was an RIC barracks in the village in which one sergeant and four constables (who were known as 'Peelers') served.

At the western end of the village is a stone monument to the O'Donnellan Clan. In 1512 Tully O'Donnellan erected a chapel which is still known as Chapel Tully. For the traveller seeking a good pint and traditional music, Broderick's Bar is recommended.

Facing page: Kilconnell Abbey Tomb (OPW)

Aughrim

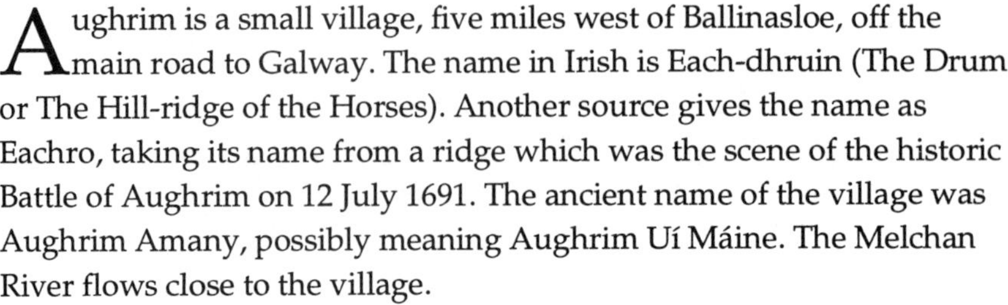

Aughrim is a small village, five miles west of Ballinasloe, off the main road to Galway. The name in Irish is Each-dhruin (The Drum or The Hill-ridge of the Horses). Another source gives the name as Eachro, taking its name from a ridge which was the scene of the historic Battle of Aughrim on 12 July 1691. The ancient name of the village was Aughrim Amany, possibly meaning Aughrim Uí Máine. The Melchan River flows close to the village.

In January 1603, Donal O'Sullivan Beara, marched from Bantry Bay with a force of a thousand people, including women and children, and reached Aughrim where they were met by a company of 800 men under Sir Thomas Burke, Lord Clanrickard's brother and Captain Malby. O'Sullivan's force made a charge, killing many of their foe including Captain Malby. O'Sullivan continued his retreat to Leitrim and reached there with only 35 people.

In 1691 the west of Ireland was still controlled by the Jacobites and one battle was to change the course of Irish history. It was an important victory by William of Orange's forces over the mainly Catholic supporters of King James II, aided by the French forces of St Ruth. Following the fall of Athlone, St Ruth made a stand on Kilcommadaun Hill, above a bog. His lines followed the high ground from the castle as far as the Tristaun Bridge. Each side had over 20,000 men. The Jacobites withstood several attacks by the Williamite army, under General de Ginkell, but a series of mistakes and misfortunes, including St Ruth's death by a cannon-ball during the battle, turned expected victory into a defeat. The conflict became known as 'The Battle of Aughrim'. According to reports, 5000 of St Ruth's army were killed and fatalities on William's side were about half that figure. The Irish retreated to Limerick where they were besieged by King William. After the battle, the bodies of the slain Irish were stripped and left unburied to be devoured by dogs and wolves.

Bloody Hollow is the location of the bloody battle between the Jacobites and Williamites. On Attidermot Hill, also known as Gallows Hill, is Aughrim Fort, a small ring fort. Following the Battle of Aughrim, William of Orange conferred the title of Viscount of Aughrim on de Ginkel and the title died out with his family. For some decades after the battle the village remained deserted and it was not until the early 1700s that the community began to grow. According to Griffith's Valuation of 1860, the population of Aughrim parish stood at 2000 with 580 in the village and 100 houses.

At the end of the eighteenth century prosperous Protestants built an orphanage for Protestant children in the village. It housed up to 25

RECOMMENDED

The Battle of Aughrim Interpretative Centre.
Finn's Pub.
St Catherine's Church.
Aughrim Castle.
Aughrim Inn.
Schoolhouse Restaurant.

children at a time and remained in operation until the 1930s. In 1839 two adults and five orphans were drowned in a boat trip on the Black Lake.

William J MacNevin was born in Aughrim in 1763 and received his early education in a hedge school. He studied in Vienna and qualified in science, medicine and continental languages. He became a member of the United Irishmen and was imprisoned. After the 1798 Rebellion he emigrated to America and was appointed to the chair of Chemistry in the College of Physicians in New York. The 34 foot MacNevin Cenotaph on Broadway is inscribed in Irish, Latin and English and dedicated to him.

The Interpretative Centre in Aughrim is given over entirely to the battle and is staffed by two very good humoured, personable guides. There is an audio visual display and a plan of the battlefield. The centre is ideally suited for tourists seeking a better knowledge of the district and for school coach tours. The centre also has a coffee shop. For those seeking something stronger there is Finn's Pub and the Aughrim Inn. Also in the vicinity is the Schoolhouse Restaurant.

Right: Memorial of site of Battle of Aughrim (OPW)
Below: Battle of Aughrim Centre

Ballinasloe

Above: Ballinasloe horse fair

RECOMMENDED

October Horse Fair.
Hayden's Hotel.
River Suck.
Route 66 Nite Club.
Leridge's County Hotel.
Grand Canal Cruising.
Olde Connaught House and Restaurant.
Angling.
Roger's Restaurant.
Pillar House Bar.
Ballinasloe Golf Club.

Ballinasloe, situated on the River Suck, is the principal market town of east Galway. The town serves as a commercial centre for the farming community and for the breeding of bloodstock on the central Plain. The name Ballinasloe means Beal Átha Sluaighe (the Town of the Ford) or Beal-Átha-na-Sluaigheadh (the Mouth of the Ford of the Hosts), showing that it was meeting place from earliest times.

Ballinasloe is a long sprawling town with many eighteenth century houses still standing in fine repair. There are several large industries in the town including Dubarry Shoes, A T Cross the quality pen manufacturer, and the French owned Square D Co. In addition over 1000 people are employed on medical services between Portiuncula Hospital and St Brigid's Psychiatric Hospital.

According to the *Annals of Innisfallen*, in 1124, Turlough O'Connor, King of Connacht, built the stone castle of Dún Leodha (which was an older name for the town) or Dunbo and a bridge to control the crossing over the River Suck. The castle became an important stronghold and, during the Elizabethan Wars, it featured in some battles. In the fourteenth century Ivy Castle was built by the O'Kellys. Later the O'Kelly clan was displaced by the Earl of Clanrickard who took control of the castle.

In the early 1650s Ireton, Cromwell's son-in-law, captured the castle and established it as the residence of the Governor of Connacht. Later Edmund Spenser took control of the estate. Early in the eighteenth century the Trench family purchased the estate from Spenser's descendants and developed an impressive town with wide streets and high buildings.

The town became the western terminus of the Grand Canal, a still water navigation, which extended from Dublin across the central plain of Ireland to join the Shannon near Banagher, with a minor branch line connecting with Ballinasloe. The Ballinasloe terminus opened in 1827. The waterway is no longer used commercially.

The Ballinasloe October Fair was the biggest horse fair in Europe, in the days of cavalry and horse transport. Originally this carnival event, with trading and music, lasted for eight days. The fair became a meeting place for farmers and traders from counties Galway, Limerick, Mayo and the Central Plain. James I granted a patent to the Earl of Clanrickard to hold a fair in the town. In 1718 Ballinasloe and the surrounding district was acquired by the Trench family (later Lords Clancarty). During the eighteenth century the new English Longhorn cattle made up much of the stock at the October Fair. Eventually, the gathering evolved into a horse fair and buyers travelled from Russia and Central

Europe to supply their armies with horses. Marengo, Napoleon's horse, which he rode at the Battle of Waterloo, was bought at the fair. The October Fair still attracts large crowds to the fair-green to buy and sell horses and enjoy the horse-jumping competitions.

In 1833 the Ballinasloe Horticultural Society for the province of Connacht was founded, under the patronage of the Earl of Clancarty, landlord of the town, who lived in Garbally Park, a mansion in a wooded demesne.

In 1842 William Makepeace Thackeray gave the following account: 'During the cattle-fair the celebrated town of Ballinasloe is thronged with farmers from all parts of the kingdom — the cattle being picturesquely exhibited in the park of the noble proprietor of the town, Lord Clancarty. As it was not fair-time, the town did not seem particularly busy, nor was there much to remark in it, except a church and a magnificent lunatic asylum, that lies outside the town on the Dublin Road; and is as handsome and stately as a palace. I think the beggars were plenteous and more loathsome here than almost anywhere; to one hideous wretch I was obliged to give money to go away, which he did for a moment, only to obtrude his horrible face directly afterwards half eaten away with disease.'

In 1824 the Earl of Clancarty built Garbally Park, a large mansion, from local stone, to the west of the town. The building is now St Joseph's College and the Catholic seminary for the diocese of Clonfert. In 1838 a Catholic chapel was erected and the following year the mental hospital, designed by Francis Johnston was built.

The Town Commissioners requested the local nuns to run the workhouse during the famine years. St Michael's Catholic church was built between 1852-58, and later it was provided with stained glass windows by Albert Power and Harry Clarke. Following the Woodford evictions of 1886, there was widespread unrest and in Ballinasloe a large demonstration was organised to greet Wilfred Blunt, an English MP, who was arrested at a protest meeting. Fr Costello, a local priest, fearing a serious clash with the police, pleaded with the crowd and they immediately returned to their homes.

The area is noted for its limestone which was once highly regarded in building circles. There are still limestone quarries in the locality.

Below: Flooding in Ballinasloe

Milltown

Milltown is a small village on the northern boundary of County Galway. It is one of the many Milltowns, Baile an Mhuilinn (The Town of the Mill) spread throughout the country. The village is situated on the banks of the River Clare which is noted for its brown trout and salmon. Like most Irish villages, it has a good variety of pubs including Ryan's and Mullarkey's. A regular feature in the district during the summer months is crossroads dancing which can be enjoyed by locals and tourists alike. In 1991 the local development association won the Ireland West Tourism Environmental Quality Award for its restoration of the old mill tank and the provision of a river walk.

Following the Anglo-Norman invasion and the conquering of Connacht, Milltown became part of the Barony of Dunmore. For a century after the invasion, Milltown was a border parish and the O'Connors and their Irish allies held out along the River Clare. Milltown as a border parish was vulnerable and subject to many wars and raids from the two greatest families in Connacht, the Clanrickard de Burgos of Galway and the McWilliam Burkes who ruled County Mayo. A border parish would be the first to be invaded and last to be evacuated. Edward Bermingham, who had been Sherrif of Mayo, built a castle beside the ford on the river, to command the crossing. The village developed around the castle. Later Bermingham built a mill to supply himself and his tenants.

The old name for Milltown parish was the Parish of Addergoole and Liskeevy which was originally two parishes. Until recent times the two churches stood in the graveyards of Liskeevy and Addergoole. The parish of Liskeevy was a long narrow strip which ran from Kilgevrin to Ballindine and to the Clare River at Milltown. Most of the boundaries were decided in the twelfth century. The present Catholic church stands in Liskeevy.

In 1598 the O'Flahertys attempted to storm Milltown Castle but Bermingham's forces kept them at bay, causing many fatalities. The O'Flahertys burned several buildings in the village and all of Bermingham's corn. They drove his cattle away towards Connemara. At Carras, the O'Flahertys were confronted by Bermingham and a British force, in the ensuing battle, the O'Flahertys were defeated and the cattle were retrieved.

The Bermingham family have had a long association with Milltown. In 1816 John Bermingham, the eminent astronomer, was born in Milltown House, close to the village. He built his own observatory in the grounds and was to write many important works on astronomy. During the period of the Penal Days Protestant landlords forbade Roman

Catholic churches on their estates but, in the early 1800s, there was a rash of building. In 1825 a church was built in Kilclooney but was replaced twelve years later by a new one in Milltown.

In the mid-1850s Michael O'Lócháin (Lohan), a disciple of Archbishop McHale, was born in the village. In 1880 he emigrated to America and the following year he launched *An Gaodhal*, the Irish language magazine for the Brooklyn Philo-Celtic Society in New York. He was a key figure of the Gaelic Revival among Irish Americans. He continued to run the magazine until his death in 1899. Michael J Molloy, the playwright, was born in Milltown on 3 March 1917. He trained for the priesthood but was never ordained. He was to become an accomplished playwright and many of his plays were produced in the Abbey Theatre. Among his best known works are *The King of Friday's Men, The Old Road* and *The Wood of the Whisperings*.

In 1879 one of the largest Land League meetings took place at Milltown, at which 15,000 people and 800 horsemen attended. In May 1884 Charles Stewart Parnell visited an estate called Kilclooney, near Milltown and purchased it for the newly formed 'The Irish Land Purchase and Settlement Company Ltd.' The company raised money by public subscription to acquire existing landed estates, which would be settled with landless men or small tenant farmers. The estate was purchased for £43,000 and the name of the village was changed to Parnellstown for a period.

There were plans to run the mail rail link between north and south Connemara through Milltown but Mr Lewin, a local landlord, living at Castlegrove, used his influence to have the line diverted to pass his own estate. The main Tuam to Claremorris road passes through the village. There are a large number of ringforts and souterrains in the area.

RECOMMENDED

Ryan's Pub.
River Clare.
Mullarkey's Pub.
Ringforts.

Right: Michael J Molloy (1917 -)

Mount Bellew

Mount Bellew is a prosperous-looking town, on the main Galway to Roscommon road, at the intersection with the Tuam to Ballinasloe road. The name in Irish is An Creagán (The Rocky Ground). Mount Bellew has been adjudged the best town in County Galway for the past number of years in the National Tidy Towns Competition. For an inland town, there are many amenities on offer for locals and tourists alike, including some pleasant walks, a picnic area, a badminton club and an 18 hole golf course. Thirsty travellers will be well catered for in the square's ten pubs. The best day to savour the atmosphere is Tuesday when a lively market is held in the square. Anything from bales of hay and livestock, to vegetables, clothes and boots can be purchased. A hairdresser even sets up business in a caravan.

The name most associated with Mount Bellew is the Bellew family. In 1655 John Bellew, a Lieutenant General, was transplanted to Connacht and granted 800 acres of land in the parishes of Moylough and Ballymoe. John Bellew's third son, Christopher, inherited his father's lands in County Galway and in 1680 his estate became known as Mount Bellew. Adjacent to his estate ran the River Shiven and he constructed a bridge over the river which later became a regular halting place for Bianconi cars on the Tuam to Ballinasloe Road. A milestone was erected on the bridge which was known as Mount Bellew Bridge, by which the town was first known until it was shortened to Mount Bellew. The exact date of the building has not been confirmed, but an estate map of 1767 shows an extensive building, surrounded by parks and gardens. The Bellews were benevolent landlords and gave much employment locally. They placed a 100 acres of their demesne under water and constructed an artificial lake. They built two bridges, an eight arch structure and an iron bridge.

Market day

In the late 1790s, during a ball at the house, a row developed between one of Bellew's sons and a member of the D'Arcy family, over a local girl. D'Arcy challenged Bellew to a duel on the lawn in front of the house. Bellew was fatally wounded and was buried by the lakeside. His family applied to the Vatican for permission to have him buried in consecrated ground. Their appeal was granted on condition that they built a church of reparation. They built the church in 1822 and the remains were buried beneath the sanctuary.

In 1824 the Franciscan friars built a monastery in the town, in which they taught pupils and trained teachers. That same year the first Mount Bellew Agricultural Show was held. In 1837 Samuel Lewis described Mount Bellew, the seat of Michael Dillon Bellew thus: 'finely situated in a demesne of 600 acres, richly wooded and embellished with an artificial lake of great beauty: in the house is a valuable collection of paintings and an extensive library.'

In March 1846 about thirty families in the nearby village of Ballinlass fell into arrears with their rents. Their landlord, Mrs Gerrard, wasn't willing to consider their pleas and evicted them. Their cottages were demolished and the families, with their humble belongings, took to the road and camped at the crossroads near Mount Bellew. Sir Henry Grattan-Bellew, an architect and engineer, on witnessing their plight offered them shelter in his stables. He later built houses for the unfortunate people. He also constructed a malt house and corn mill and encouraged his tenants to grow corn, which he bought from them. He reversed the flow of the river to operate the mill wheel. Bellew was also responsible for designing the square and a similar one in Tyrrellspass.

In 1904, on the recommendation of the Archbishop of Tuam, the Franciscans opened Mount Bellew Agricultural College to train young farmers. Early in the twentieth century the Mount Bellew Agricultural Co-Operative was established, with Sir Henry Grattan-Bellew and Brother Joseph Daly of the Franciscans as principal founders. Their most important project was the building of a new mill between 1917-22, close to the bridge. Besides milling corn and maize, it provided employment for locals. Another new development was the opening of a saw mill. In 1921 an electricity plant was built, powered by water from the River Shiven. The *Tuam Herald* reported: 'Mount Bellew was possibly one of the first districts of its size in Ireland to have an electric plant installed.' In 1924 a fierce fire destroyed the mill but it was quickly rebuilt and still thrives to-day.

In 1937 the Bellews sold their house and estate to the Irish Land Commission who divided the land among local farmers. Two years later the house was demolished and the stones were used to repair the roads in the Moylough/Mount Bellew area.

Worth a visit is The Square Kitchen Coffee Shop which has old Singer sewing machines as tables. There is an interesting walk from the church alongside the wildlife sanctuary and lake.

RECOMMENDED

Mount Bellew Golf Club.
Grattan Club.
Holy Rosary College.
The Square Kitchen Coffee Shop.
Lake View Restaurant.
Forge Museum.
Mount Bellew Historical Society.
Mount Bellew Badminton Club.
Market (Tuesday).
St Mary's Church.
Bird Sanctuary.
Agricultural College.

MOUNTBELLEW

Moylough

Moylough is a small village about four miles from Mount Bellew on the road to Tuam. The name in Irish is Maigh Locha (The Plain of the Lake). The village is central to the Corrib and Suck River system and is popular with game and coarse anglers. One of the most prominent features of the district is a number of ruined castles.

In the late twelfth century the Anglo-Normans established a settlement in Moylough. At the time most of the area was under forests. The Cogeshale family were granted large tracts of land in Connacht by Meiler de Bermingham. They built Moylough Castle. Over two miles northwest of the castle there was another small castle in the townland of Moat.

In the thirteenth century the Carr family ran a linen weaving industry in the locality. The de Bermingham family required linen for their castle and asked the Carrs to supply it. The Carrs refused and their looms were shut down. Following discussions, the Carrs agreed to trade linen for a windmill. With the decline of the linen trade, the Carrs turned to farming and ground corn in the windmill.

In 1819 John O'Rourke, a magistrate, noted for handing down stiff sentences to anyone who appeared in his court, lived in the vicinity. O'Rourke and a force of soldiers set an ambush for a group of Ribbonmen (a secret society). They opened fire and killed many of them. In 1820 O'Rourke sentenced two Ribbonmen, Ned Lohan and James Tyrell, to death for their part in the murder of his colleague, Edward Browne, in Moylough. Despite many attempts to assassinate O'Rourke, he remained in Moylough until his death in 1849.

During the Penal Days, priests dressed in old peasant clothes and celebrated Mass in a hollow field close to Aghiart. They hid their vessels in the fields. In 1834 Archbishop McHale of Tuam realised the dangers to the Catholic Church of the Proselytising Societies and gave the Franciscans eleven foundations in the diocese including one in Moylough, in an effort to prevent the societies spreading. That same year a National Schools' Survey reported that there were three hedge schools in the village. In 1836 Samuel Lewis stated that Moylough was head of a Union of Roman Catholic parishes called Aghiart comprising the parishes of Moylough, Aghiart and Killascobe with a church in each parish.

RECOMMENDED

Moylough Castle.
Moylough Brass and Reed Band.
St Patrick's Church.
Wedge Tomb.

For centuries the two half parishes, of Moylough and Mount Bellew, were completely separate but, at the beginning of the nineteenth century, both communities, together with Killascobe, were united as one parish. In 1848 Killascobe broke away to become the parish of Menlough, and the parish of Moylough/Mount Bellew, then came into being. The following year St Patrick's Catholic Church in Moylough was built on land donated by Christopher Dillon Bellew. There are no deeds or leases in existence for the church. The only provision for its upkeep was an annual collection known as the 'Seats' Collection'. Since 1964 the church has been renovated.

There was a strong tradition in the 1850s to celebrate St John's Eve, on the 23rd June with the lighting of bonfires. On 23 June 1872 an effigy of the despised Judge William Keogh was hung, drawn and quartered before being burned on the bonfire. Judge Keogh made vigorous attacks on the Catholic clergy and had handed down severe sentences for minor offences.

There are several pleasant walks in the vicinity and outside the village lies a lake in the townland of Laught, with swimming facilities. A 4000-year-old wedge tomb is to be found in the townland of Kilbeg.

Below: Moylough Castle

Dunmore

The small village of Dunmore is north-east of Moylough, on the Tuam to Ballyhaunis Road. The name in Irish is Dún Mór (Big Fort), which derives its name from the great fort of Turlough O'Connor, King of Connacht and High King of Ireland (1106-56). The territory, stretching from Milltown to the Roscommon border, was called Conmaic ne Dunmore, presumably because its chief resided at the Great Fort from which the name of the village evolved.

The village is situated on the Sinking River, with a market square, consisting of many pubs and shops still retaining old traditional shop fronts. There is a good selection of pubs for the weary traveller to choose from including The Four Seasons, Byrne's, The Emerald and O'Connors for music sessions. Along with the castle, the other landmark worth visiting is the Augustinian Abbey.

It is reputed that Conmaic ne Dunmore was established by the O'Flahertys as a buffer stronghold against their most powerful rivals in Connacht, the O'Connors, on the north-east and the Kellys of Hy Maine on the south-east. There was continued unrest in this area, as the three families fought over it. Finally in 1106 King Turlough O'Connor defeated the Conmaic ne force. The O'Connors held the territory, until it was conquered by the Anglo-Normans at the beginning of the thirteenth century. In 1230 William de Burgo granted the Barony of Dunmore to the de Bermingham family, who built the present Dunmore Castle in 1247 on the site of the old O'Connor fort. By 1280 a small town, enclosed by walls, had developed beside the castle. The warring tribes of the O'Flahertys and O'Connors repeatedly attacked the Norman stronghold of Dunmore.

About 1425 Walter de Bermingham, Lord Baron of Athenry and Dunmore, established a priory for the Augustinian Eremites. The ruins of the Augustinian Abbey still stand in the village. The lovely fifteenth century doorway, the holy water stoup and the early Christian cross inside are all worthy of note. West of the priory is a mound at Knockmannanan, known as King Turlough's Grave. According to Sir William Petty's map of 1658 the name of the village appears as Downamore, suggesting that it might have been originally Domhnach, deriving from St Patrick's monastery believed to have been built nearby.

In 1837 Samuel Lewis's *Topographical Dictionary of Ireland* stated: 'The Roman Catholic parish, co-extensive with that of the established church, had a small slated chapel. 400 children were educated in two public schools and 260 in eight private establishments.' In 1848 the author, Anthony Trollope, lived in Dunmore for a period and set his novel *The Kellys and the O'Kellys* in the village. In June 1859 the McDonnells, a

RECOMMENDED

Dunmore Castle.
Augustinian Abbey.
Shrule Monastic Site.
Market Square.
Sinking River.
The Four Seasons Pub.
Thomas Byrne's Pub.
O'Connor's Pub (food and music).
Dunmore Golf Driving Range.
Dunmore Heritage Symposium (August).

merchant family originally from Glencoe in Scotland, purchased the Boyounagh estate in Dunmore. A striking Celtic cross marks their burial place.

In 1920 the Black and Tans were based in Dunmore and sought out Volunteers and 'men on the run'. They would question and intimidate local men, especially on market day. The Volunteers destroyed the bridge between Dunmore and Glenamaddy, restricting the movement of the Tans.

In the surrounding countryside and townlands, there are many archaeological remains, most notably ringforts at Killnalapa and Roymonaghan. There are several associations with St Patrick, including a holy well at Cappagh and the Shrule monastic site, an early Christian site with the remains of a small church, a Bullaun stone or St Patrick's stone (used for grinding corn or as a holy water font), a Tau Cross and children's Burial Ground (often found in places like this or in ringforts, unbaptised children are buried there or near running water to keep evil spirits at bay). There are ancient monastic sites at Killooney and Addergoole and a dolmen at Garrafrauns. Today Dunmore Heritage Centre offers a comprehensive guide to the many historical and archaeological sites in the parish and gives guided tours.

Some interesting characters had associations with Dunmore. Gideon Ouseley, who became a Methodist preacher, was born in the village and travelled extensively throughout Ireland, preaching the gospel in Irish. He died on 14 May 1839. John Reilly, the blind piper, lived most of his life in Dunmore and taught the famous McPeake family of Belfast to play the fiddle. From the top of Checker Hill (northeast of the village) you can view a radius of forty miles over Mayo, Roscommon and Galway.

Right: Augustinian Abbey (Dunmore Community Heritage Committee)

Glenamaddy

Glenamaddy is a picturesque rural village situated in the north-east corner of County Galway. The village is located in a predominantly limestone region and a large turlough (a seasonal lake) and two lakes dominate the landscape to the south. The name in Irish is Gleann na Madadh, (derived from the Irish word, 'Gleann' for a valley and 'madadh' from 'madra', for a dog, Valley of the Dogs or Glen of the Curs). According to Rev Walter Conway, the name is Gleann-na-Maighe-Duibh (the Valley of the Black Plain). The old name for the parish of Glenamaddy was Boyounagh (Yellow River). It is reputed that St Patrick visited Glenamaddy and founded the first church in Boyounagh around which an early Christian site developed. In later years the Dominicans built a priory close to the original site.

Glenamaddy is an attractive village, where four roads meet and it has been immortalised in song, *The Four Country Roads.* The buildings are freshly painted with many shops still retaining old style fronts. The two banks are tastefully located in old converted buildings. One of the most impressive buildings in the village is St Patrick's Catholic Church. It is well worth a visit to view the Harry Clarke stained glass windows and the old baptismal font. For the thirsty traveller, The Four Roads Pub or the Oakland Hotel can be recommended.

In the thirteenth century Kiltullagh Castle was built beside the lake by the Concannon family, who were one of the branches of the O'Connor clan. Only the ruins of the castle remain today. Close to the castle is a holy well, an ancient graveyard and the ruins of Kiltullagh church.

Glenamaddy did not develop until the 1820s, when regular markets were held in the village. In 1853 the workhouse was built in the village and housed up to 600 inmates. It was a traditional building with a forbidding appearance but was small in size and white-washed. In 1885 the Bon Secours Sisters of Dublin were asked to take charge of the overcrowded workhouse. In 1926 the workhouse was closed and the occupants were transferred to St Mary's Home in Tuam. After 'The Troubles', the hospital section served as an orphanage and later the district dispensary.

In 1904 St Patrick's gothic style Catholic Church was built to replace a smaller more primitive edifice built in 1820. In 1909 St Bridget's Town Hall was built by Fr Conway and it played a central role in the cultural and social life of the parish. In 1920 the building was burnt by the Black and Tans but was rebuilt by the community. The building is now being restored, to include a theatre, heritage and exhibition centre with music. In 1924 Joe Gilmore built a mill and it gave badly needed employment in

RECOMMENDED

Heritage Centre.
Jeremiah Mee Memorial.
Glenamaddy Craft Shop.
St Patrick's Church.
Pitch and Putt Course.
Oakland Hotel.
Crannóg-Kiltullagh Lake.
The Four Roads Pub.
Ringforts.
The All-Ireland Confined Drama Finals (April).
Glenamaddy Arts and Historical Society.
Four Roads Festival (July).

the locality. It operated until the early 1960s when it was unable to compete with a local co-operative.

The area is rich in antiquities. Four miles north of Glenamaddy a megalithic tomb can be found in the townland of Ballinastack. Another place of interest is the crannóg on Kiltullagh Lake which dates to the late Bronze Age. Closeby there is one of the most impressive ringforts in the area.

Glenamaddy boasts of a long tradition of music and drama. The Esker Ballroom which opened in 1949, was one of the most popular dance venues in the county. At the height of the showband era of the 1960s and 70s, Glenamaddy was the mecca for dancing in north-east Galway. All the popular bands played regularly at 'The Sound of Music' Ballroom. Each April, since 1960, the Glenamaddy Dramatic Society has played host to the All-Ireland Confined Drama Festival, with participating drama groups from throughout Ireland. The Festival attracts large crowds to the village.

There is a memorial to Jeremiah Mee, on the Ballymoe Road at the Glenamaddy crossroads. Mee was born in Glenamaddy in 1889 and became famous as a young RIC constable in the Listowel Mutiny of 1920, when he refused to serve in the proposed new force of combined RIC and Black and Tans. He served as Secretary to Countess Markievitz, in the Department of Labour in the Dail. He died in 1953.

Below: Bog Cotton (Irish Peatland Conservation Council)

Eamon Ceannt, one of the seven signatories of the Proclamation of the Republic, Easter Week 1916, was born in Glenamaddy on 21 September 1881. He was a well educated young man and taught classes in Irish. Ceannt became involved in the Republican movement and assisted with the Howth gun-running. In Easter Week 1916 he commanded the 4th Battalion of the Irish Volunteers, which occupied the South Dublin Union. Ceannt was executed by firing squad in Kilmainham Jail, Dublin, on 8 May 1916.

East of the village is Loch Lurgeen, a raised bog of particular significance to those interested in the flora and fauna of wetlands, including David Bellamy, the noted television nature expert. Glennamaddy is twinned with Guiscriff in Brittany and people from both places have exchanged visits.

INDEX